Reading and Language Arts Programs

Essential Tools for Educators

The Program Evaluation Guides for Schools

Richard M. Jaeger, Series Editor

Mary W. Olson
Samuel D. Miller

Reading and Language Arts Programs

A Guide to Evaluation

The Program Evaluation Guides for Schools
Series Editor: Richard M. Jaeger

CORWIN PRESS, INC.
A Sage Publications Company
Newbury Park, California 91320

For information address:

Corwin Press, Inc.
A Sage Publications Company
2455 Teller Road
Newbury Park, California 91320

SAGE Publications Ltd.
6 Bonhill Street
London EC2A 4PU
United Kingdom

SAGE Publications India Pvt. Ltd.
M-32 Market
Greater Kailash I
New Delhi 110 048 India

Printed in the United States of America

Library of Congress Cataloging-in-Publication Data
Olson, Mary W.
    Reading and language arts programs: a guide to evaluation / Mary
W. Olson, Samuel D. Miller.
        p. cm.   — (Essential tools for educators)
    Includes bibliographical references and index.
    ISBN 0-8039-6042-5
    1. Language arts (Elementary)—Evaluation. 2. Language arts
(Secondary)—Evaluation. 3. Reading (Elementary)—Evaluation.
4. Reading (Secondary)—Evaluation. I. Miller, Samuel D.
II. Title. III. Series.
LB1576.045 1993
428'.0071—dc20   92-37084

The paper in this book meets the specifications for permanence of the American National Standards Institute and the National Association of State Textbook Administrators.

93 94 95 96 10 9 8 7 6 5 4 3 2 1

Corwin Press Production Editor: Tara S. Mead

Contents

Series Editor's Preface

Essential Tools for Educators: The Program Evaluation Guides for Schools is a series grounded in the premise that regular evaluation of school programs can be of enormous help to school professionals—provided *they* are the ones who plan the evaluations, conduct the evaluations, and use the evaluations to guide their school improvement activities. Evaluation is a powerful tool for documenting school needs, identifying strengths and weaknesses in school programs, and discovering how to improve almost every aspect of school life. Program evaluation need not be complex or inordinately time-consuming. Simple principles and strategies are described in the initial volume of this series, *Evaluating School Programs: An Educator's Guide*. Then, specific techniques and approaches are illustrated in the program-focused guides that complete the series. Using these principles and techniques, teachers, principals, and other school professionals *can* plan, conduct, and interpret the findings of powerful evaluations of their curricula; of their instructional programs in mathematics, reading, language arts, and special education; of their programs for "at-risk" students; and of their counseling and personnel development programs. The principles to be learned from this series can be applied even more broadly to the evaluation of school disciplinary programs, student assessment programs, community relations programs, and other programmatic elements that are central to the successful functioning of a school.

Extensive technical training is *not* prerequisite to planning and conducting sound evaluations of school programs. Sound evaluation *does* require a desire to improve one's school, willingness to work collegially, careful attention to detail, and basic knowledge of how school program evaluations should be carried out. The ETE series provides school professionals with the last of these elements—the essential tools they need to plan and conduct effective evaluations of their school programs.

Evaluating School Programs: An Educator's Guide is the foundation volume in this series. It contains a clear, concise exposition of the objectives, principles, and core issues that undergird solid evaluations of school programs. By reading this guide, teachers, principals, and their colleagues will learn how to (a) determine the feasibility of conducting a school program evaluation, (b) focus a school program evaluation, (c) structure and design a school program evaluation, (d) conduct a school program evaluation, (e) interpret the results of a school program evaluation, (f) report and make use of the results of a school program evaluation, and (g) ensure that a school program evaluation is conducted ethically, damages no one, and enriches all who are associated with the program being evaluated.

Once these basic elements of a school evaluation are well understood, readers will be ready to proceed to the guide in this series that focuses on the subject area of the program to be evaluated. Each program-specific guide provides specific instruction on the evaluation of school programs in a single subject area, and each follows a consistent pattern of organization. Following an introduction that provides an overview and rationale for program evaluation in its subject area, each program-specific guide contains a sequence of vignettes (chapters) that illustrate, in detail, evaluation of a focused aspect of a school program. Collectively, these vignettes illustrate how evaluations of school programs are planned, structured, staffed, conducted, interpreted, and used. The vignettes cover a wide range of practical evaluative issues; illustrate the selection, development, and use of a large number of evaluation strategies and instruments; and show how the results of evaluation can be used to strengthen school programs. Resources at the end of each program-specific guide contain a set of research-based standards and indicators of school program quality, a road map to the use of these standards in evaluating the effectiveness and efficiency of a school program, and an annotated bibliography of selected references on program evaluation in the subject area of the guide.

Evaluations can help school professionals make their school the best it can be and, in the process, substantially increase their own educational effectiveness. In the hands of thoughtful, well-trained school professionals, evaluation can be a transformative catalyst that improves schools and all who work and learn in them. The ETE series will help you become one of those distinctive school professionals who can make school program evaluations work well. Knowing that your investment in this knowledge will pay rich dividends for years to come, I wish you every success.

RICHARD M. JAEGER
University of North Carolina,
Greensboro

About the Authors

Samuel D. Miller is Associate Professor at the University of North Carolina at Greensboro, where he teaches courses in reading, language arts, and educational psychology. He was an elementary classroom teacher for 10 years. He received his M.Ed. in Elementary Education from Rhode Island College and his Ph.D. in Curriculum and Psychological Studies from the University of Michigan. His research focuses on students' literacy development and motivation at the elementary and middle school levels. His publications have appeared in the *Journal of Educational Psychology, JRB: A Journal of Literacy,* and the *Elementary School Journal.* His professional service activities include serving as a member of various International Reading Association and National Reading Conference committees and as an advisory board member for several professional journals.

Mary W. Olson is Professor at the University of North Carolina at Greensboro, where she is the Associate Dean of the School of Education and teaches courses in reading and language arts. She has worked with school districts in Texas, Oklahoma, Illinois, Florida, and North Carolina, consulting with them on such issues as program evaluation, beginning reading, vocabulary and comprehension development, and writing. Her professional experiences include 13 years as a classroom teacher in diverse roles, teaching in self-contained classrooms, open schools, and Chapter I programs, and serving as a middle school reading specialist. Her publications include book chapters in leading textbooks, reports of studies of writing, spelling, and reading processes, and practitioner-oriented articles in leading reading and language arts journals. She is editor of *Opening the Door to Classroom Research* and coeditor of *Teacher to Teacher: Strategies for the Elementary Classroom.* She received the first outstanding teaching award at Southwest Texas State University. Her professional service activities include serving as a member of various International Reading Association (IRA) committees and as chair of the International Reading Association's NCATE Advisory Group; Secretary of the National Reading Conference;

President, Treasurer, and Secretary of the Texas State Reading Association; and editorial consultant for several professional journals. She completed her Ph.D. in Curriculum and Instruction at the University of Texas at Austin, her M.Ed. in Reading at Southwest Texas State University, and her B.A. in Elementary Education at Trinity University.

Introduction

This guide is intended to help school personnel design and conduct evaluations of language arts and reading programs. Specifically, it is designed for teachers in K-12 classrooms, reading and language arts supervisors or coordinators, school principals, and assistant principals who see a need to evaluate their instructional programs. In other words, practitioners (and, perhaps, outside evaluators) will benefit from this guide, which is one of a series of program evaluation guides. In this series, *Evaluating School Programs: An Educator's Guide* provides a broad introduction to program evaluation while the program-specific guides illustrate evaluation of specific school programs. This guide targets the evaluation of language arts and reading programs.

This Guide Is for You   Because this guide is intended to help classroom teachers and building-level administrators in designing and conducting evaluations of their school's reading and language arts programs, readers do not need an advanced degree in program evaluation to understand the principles and procedures discussed. Our intended audience is classroom teachers and administrators in individual schools who might be involved in an evaluation of their reading and language arts programs. This guide centers on improvement of language arts and reading programs through focused evaluations that are planned and conducted by school personnel. No external accountability requirement or motivation is assumed.

Why Evaluate Language Arts and Reading Programs?

Among other purposes, program evaluations are used to determine the effectiveness of programs, the adequacy of current resources, the need for additional resources, necessary program changes or modifications, or the relevance of a program to a particular school's needs. The results of program evaluations may influence decisions at the school, district, or state level concerning funding, recognition, and long-range planning for language arts and reading programs. Consider the following scenarios.

Scenarios for Evaluation

Scenario 1. You are the assistant principal in a school with a substantial number of at-risk students. For the last two years, the special education teachers in your school have attended inservice workshops aimed at improving the reading and language arts curricula for the at-risk students assigned to Chapter I and special education programs. They have worked extremely hard, and they appear to have been quite successful implementing new strategies for those children. Fewer students are being referred for special education placements, and test scores of students who attend resource rooms have improved steadily. Your principal wants to capitalize on the program's success, yet funds in the district are limited. At the local council meeting of the International Reading Association, you learn of new federal funds for successful programs for at-risk students that might be expanded. To be eligible, you have to document your program's successful components and how you would strengthen, modify, or change them.

Scenario 2. The state legislature mandated the evaluation of the state's public schools to identify schools with low student achievement. During the subsequent evaluation, your school's student achievement level was lower than the state average. One of the significantly weak areas in your school's performance was students' reading and language arts test scores. Your district's superintendent is very concerned about making the necessary modifications to, additions to, or deletions from the reading and language arts program, but you, as the principal, do not know which components of the program should be retained, which should be changed, or which should be abandoned. You do, however, recognize that the school's reading and language arts program must be the object of in-depth evaluation to provide guidance for any intelligent changes.

Scenario 3. Based on information in professional journals, you and other language arts and reading teachers are concerned that your middle school's language arts and reading program does not encourage or provide students with opportunities to read for enjoyment or for learning subject material. Reading continuous text provides students with practice in higher-order thinking skills and time to experience or express affective responses as they experience different genres. You and your fellow teachers are aware that a number of alternative causes could be attributed to the students' perceived low rate of reading continuous text; therefore you have proposed a formative evaluation to examine the nature of the language arts and reading program, specifically the program components related to reading extended texts for various purposes.

Scenario 4. You are a science teacher in the local high school and also the head of the science department. Two years ago, your school began a Writing Across the Curriculum program in response to teachers' concerns about the poor writing abilities of the school's students. Because the program has been in place for two years, you believe an evaluation of the program would be timely for several reasons. First, you wonder if student writing has improved in the past two years. Second, a related concern is whether or not all of the teachers in the high school participated in the program. Third, even though you know the science department's faculty participated, you do not know if the science teachers were particularly skilled in their implementation of the program.

Reasons for Program Evaluations   The reasons that program evaluations were needed in each of the above scenarios were straightforward. Teachers and administrators in the first scenario needed to document the strengths and weaknesses of the program for at-risk students to be eligible for additional funds to expand the program. In the second scenario, the principal of the school needed to determine what changes she might make to improve her school's student achievement. In the third scenario, the teachers believed they had identified a program weakness and needed an evaluation to examine their belief and subsequently make any necessary changes. The science teacher in the fourth scenario had several concerns about the effectiveness of the Writing Across the Curriculum program that only a program evaluation could adequately address. If program evaluations were not conducted in these scenarios, it would be difficult for the teachers or administrators to make decisions about what worked and why. It would also be difficult, if not impossible, to make decisions about how available resources should be used in the best possible way, how to obtain additional funds, or whether to retain any or all parts of a particular program.

Ongoing evaluations of reading and language arts programs can be useful in many situations and for many reasons (see Sanders's *Evaluating School Programs: An Educator's Guide,* Chapter 1, in the Essential Tools for Educators series). They are especially needed for the following reasons:

- to develop language arts and reading curricula that are suited to a particular school and student body (for example, children from families with a low literacy level might need a program with a major focus on the forms and functions of print early in their school experiences)

- to determine the adequacy of current resources for students and/or the need for additional student resources in a language arts and reading program, such as books of various genres
- to determine what instructional changes or modifications are needed in a language arts and reading program given a program's goals
- to assess students' language arts and reading achievement in ways beyond the traditional standardized test format and level of thinking (standardized tests are often considered an artificial context to evaluate the thinking and decision making students must do to read and/or write extended text)
- to determine the worth of particular components of a language arts and reading program (for example, this may mean considering one aspect of the reading curriculum or perhaps a new intervention strategy in the writing curriculum)

What Is the Philosophy Underlying This Guide?

This guide is based on three beliefs about program evaluation. First, we believe that school personnel such as teachers, service-delivery personnel, and school administrators can improve the quality of instructional programs, particularly language arts and reading programs, by examining these programs in a systematic way using criteria that have been found to characterize effective and successful language arts and reading programs. Evaluation is a tool for all school professionals to help them improve their programs, secure the resources they need, support sound advocacy claims, modify policies affecting language arts and reading curriculum, and work together more effectively.

Philosophy Underlying This Guide

Second, we believe that program evaluation should be planned and conducted as a generative activity of school personnel, not as a responsive activity. School personnel should evaluate language arts and reading programs on their own terms and for their own purposes. In the four scenarios that introduced this guide, school personnel had specific purposes for initiating the evaluations. They were not evaluating as a result of an outside mandate to evaluate.

Third, we believe teachers and supervisors of language arts and reading programs can develop the knowledge and skills to conduct useful evaluations. To organize and conduct a sound evaluation of a language arts and reading program, you do not need advanced courses in statistics or evaluation. Nor do you need to use sophisticated statistical procedures or fancy research techniques. *Evaluating School Programs: An Educator's Guide* and this guide contain information to help you conduct a carefully planned and systematic evaluation of your school programs. Because we believe evaluation of language arts and reading programs should be a tool for school personnel, we obviously believe they can learn how to conduct a sound evaluation.

What Is in This Guide?

This guide is divided into four major sections. The first is the introduction that you are currently reading. It includes information on the purposes of the guide, why it is useful to evaluate language arts and reading programs, the philosophy underlying the guide, what the guide contains, how to use the guide, how to conduct a program evaluation, and some general cautions on program evaluation. In fact, this introduction orients the reader to the guide as well as to the evaluation of language arts and reading programs.

How This Guide Is Organized

The second major section of the guide provides six vignettes, or examples, of program evaluations in schools. These vignettes include information about data collection strategies, data collection instruments, examples of evaluation results and their interpretation, and alternatives to data collection methods. Specifically, the series of vignettes illustrates the decision-making process that is necessary when conducting program evaluations. The vignettes were written to create a context with which readers might identify and thus follow the procedures described in the vignettes. The vignettes illustrate contexts for evaluation at the elementary, middle/junior high, and senior high school levels. Their settings vary and include schools in rural, suburban, inner-city, and small town locations; the student populations are also diverse with respect to students' racial composition and socioeconomic and achievement status. In each vignette, the school setting, the reasons for evaluating a component of the language arts and reading program, and the persons involved in the evaluation are described. Each vignette also notes the advantages and disadvantages of using particular approaches to data collection, how data collection instruments are created and data are collected, how to interpret evaluation results, and how to present those results. We concluded each vignette with a summary of the evaluation principles represented in the vignette, evaluation alternatives that could have been used, and some cautions regarding interpretation of the results. Our purpose was to provide readers with real life scenarios of how and why language arts and reading programs might be evaluated to enhance readers' conceptual understanding of program evaluation across the K-12 spectrum. As stated earlier, our intent was to present practical and feasible vignettes that would help school personnel design and conduct their own program evaluations. We believe the evaluations we described are well within the capabilities of most classroom teachers and administrators.

Indicators of Quality

The third major section of this guide is Resource A, which lists standards and indicators of high quality reading and language arts programs in schools, together with suggested data collection instruments for each indicator. They were selected using two criteria. First, the standards and indicators were developed from an extensive review of the reading and language arts literature. Any standard or indicator included in Resource A was based on empirical support from the research literature. Second, because it was assumed that evaluative data would be collected within individual schools, any standard or indicator included in Resource A can be measured adequately with the resources available to most schools.

As we prepared this guide, decisions had to be made about which standards and indicators as well as which language arts and reading curricular components would be used to illustrate evaluation principles in the vignettes. These decisions were based on discussions with school personnel, who gave the highest priority to the examples that are presented. First, we selected standards and indicators that would show a wide variety of data collection approaches, data collection procedures, and methods for organizing, analyzing, and reporting results. We included two types of checklists, student and teacher interviews, a time log, questionnaires, and portfolios. Second, curricular components (e.g., writing assignments, reading comprehension) that seemed to have the greatest appeal to teachers at a variety of grade levels were selected.

The final section of the guide is Resource B, a bibliography that is divided into four sections: reading, writing, listening, and speaking. The bibliography contains examples of program evaluations, particularly language arts and reading program evaluations, and references to help school personnel select data collection instruments, such as articles on portfolio assessment. Readers may wish to refer to these additional sources of information.

Program Evaluation Versus Program Implementation and Research

At this point, we would like to describe what is not in this guide by contrasting program *evaluation* with program *implementation* and *research*. This guide does not include information for teachers on how to implement high quality reading and language arts programs. We believe this is the goal of instructional leaders, reading and language arts methods courses, or inservice programs. Nor does the guide offer suggestions on how to conduct research; it only offers suggestions related to program evaluations. Evaluations are designed to secure specific information about a particular program. Research is designed to study a representative few so as to generalize to the many and must be governed by certain assumptions. The conditions that must be present in research that enable results to be generalized to other settings or populations are not required in evaluations. In fact, the demands of being able to generalize information to other programs, students, or schools is a characteristic of research that is less important in program evaluation. We view generalizing conclusions to other settings and populations to be a major purpose of *research,* whereas many program evaluations limit generalization to a particular setting. This should not imply that evaluations should not be conducted systematically and thoroughly. Program evaluation is presented as a process in which evidence is obtained, analyzed, and synthesized into relevant information for decision making; moreover, evaluation results, like research results, are only as valid as the methods used to gather them.

How to Use This Guide

Evaluating School Programs: An Educator's Guide, and each program-specific guide in this series, has a table of contents to help readers locate information. The table of contents for this guide includes an introduction, the six vignettes, a resource for data sources and data collection instruments, a list of standards and indicatiors, and a list of selected references divided into the language arts components of reading, writing, listening, and speaking. For example, if readers want to see an example of a program evaluation for a particular component of a reading/language arts curriculum, they could check the table of contents to determine which vignettes are available for the respective component. Or, if readers want to determine possible data collection instruments for particular standards and indicators, they could consult Table A.1, which illustrates data collection strategies for the standards and indicators listed in Resource A.

Using *Evaluating School Programs: An Educator's Guide* and This Guide

As readers respond to the purpose of this guide, which is to assist school personnel in designing and conducting evaluations of their school's language arts and reading programs, they will have varying degrees of expertise in program evaluation. We expect readers of the guide to fall into one of three categories: readers who know nothing about program evaluation, readers who have some knowledge of program evaluation, and readers who are fairly knowledgeable about program evaluations.

For readers who know nothing about program evaluation, we recommend first reading *Evaluating School Programs: An Educator's Guide.* It provides readers with a rationale for evaluating school programs as well as guidance on how to focus an evaluation, collect information about a program, organize and analyze the information, report information, and administer a program evaluation. The next step for novice program evaluators is to read carefully the Introduction to this guide, which will help orient them to evaluating language arts and reading programs. Finally, read the six vignettes in this guide that were especially created for evaluating language arts and reading programs.

For readers who are somewhat familiar with program evaluation, we recommend briefly reviewing *Evaluating School Programs: An Educator's Guide.* We suggest particular attention to the sections on collecting information, organizing and analyzing information, and reporting information. With this review in mind, the next step is to read the Introduction and vignettes in this guide, because the vignettes offer a variety of contexts from which readers might gain ideas for their own program evaluations.

Finally, for readers who are knowledgeable about program evaluation, we suggest using this guide as a resource book as needed. The Introduction and vignettes will be helpful as you plan to evaluate your language arts and reading program.

What Should I Evaluate?

Because language arts and reading program evaluations are conducted to answer particular questions or concerns, the program components to be evaluated are determined by those concerns or questions about the program. Each of this guide's vignettes was written to show how various concerns or questions were transformed into decisions about what to evaluate.

Focusing an Evaluation

Whatever evaluation plans you make for your language arts and reading program, we suggest that only one component of the program be evaluated at a time. Accomplishing this feat necessitates assigning priorities to concerns. For instance, evaluating the writing aspect of the language arts program might mean determining whether to evaluate opportunities for students to understand the writing process or perhaps evaluating actual student compositions or even teachers' writing assignments. Certainly, trying to evaluate more than one program component at a time could prove too time consuming for a school's staff.

How Will I Conduct the Evaluation?

Thoughtful planning can eliminate many unnecessary problems when conducting a program evaluation. Thoughtful planning requires consideration of why the program is being evaluated, what the evaluation should produce, and who will see the results. Specifying *why* a program is being evaluated will assist the evaluation team when defining the scope of their investigation, preparing to collect data, and choosing which staff members will be involved. Specifying *what* the evaluation of a program will produce will help when determining how to collect data, who will be involved in data collection, and how long the process will take. Specifying *who* will see the evaluation's results will help when determining how to organize results and their interpretation. Adequate consideration of these issues via reflective planning at the outset will save much time, energy, and resources.

Steps in Using This Guide

Implicit in each vignette are the general steps one follows when conducting a program evaluation. The format we used as we wrote each vignette illustrates the planning that is involved when conducting program evaluations. Each vignette starts with a description of a particular school and a discussion about a concern or question the school personnel have about some component of the reading and language arts program. Issues are raised to explain the different reasons for conducting a program evaluation. At this point in the vignette, a chairperson and committee are selected to guide the evaluation. Their first step is to narrow the evaluation's focus by selecting a standard and indicator(s) from the standards and indicators that are listed in Resource A. The standard selected should reflect the area of concern.

As soon as the committee decides on a standard and indicator(s) that reflect the area of concern, issues that surround program evaluation must be examined. These issues are related primarily to the school's resources and the reasons that an evaluation is needed. Remember that programs may be evaluated because teachers are concerned about a particular problem; for example, perhaps the principal has received parents' complaints about a language arts or reading issue, or the school faculty is concerned about test scores. The audience for each of these problems will have a different set of expectations that need to be understood and addressed. Another issue that warrants serious consideration by an evaluation committee is available resources, a factor that will influence that manner in which data are collected. A school's choice of data collection strategies will be influenced by its available resources of money, time, and staff.

Using Available Resources

At this point, school personnel may ask themselves, "How can we know how resources will affect a program evaluation before we even begin?" We realize that school personnel cannot predict everything, yet we cannot emphasize enough the need for planning. We hope that schools will have enough resources to address adequately all essential steps in the evaluation process. School personnel surely need to understand how these factors could affect an evaluation prior to beginning one.

Collecting, Organizing, Analyzing, and Reporting the Evaluation Results

As the evaluation committee considers these factors, they should investigate a variety of alternative data collection strategies, each of which has its own advantages and disadvantages (these are discussed in the vignettes). In selecting a strategy, the committee must decide what data they need, how the data will be collected, who will collect it, and how confidentiality will be ensured. They will also determine how the evaluation results will be analyzed and presented to the administration and/or faculty.

In the vignettes, we attempted to be as realistic as possible and not assume resources that were beyond the reach of most schools; consequently, we suggest that school personnel, likewise, should be realistic when they plan their evaluations. We also strongly recommend that school personnel create an evaluation plan based on the steps outlined in this guide prior to embarking on a program evaluation. A step-by-step plan takes time, yet it can save much time later. Many problems can be anticipated and avoided as a result of planning. Without planning, school personnel may not obtain the information needed to address their initial concerns and might find their evaluation efforts to be largely ineffective.

Summary

In this introduction, we have presented a number of reasons for conducting program evaluations of language arts and reading curricula. We have explained the philosophy behind this guide as well as the scope of the guide. We discussed what is in this guide and how it is organized. Finally, we explained how to use the guide. In the following series of vignettes that describe evaluations of components of reading and language arts programs, the issues we raised in this introduction are illustrated within specific contexts. In addition, we provide standards and indicators of quality reading and language arts programs with suggested data gathering instruments for each indicator (Resource A). Sources listed in the bibliography (Resource B) at the end of this guide provide additional resources.

1

Vignette One

Evaluation of Library Resources

Where, What, and Why?

Roger Williams Elementary School is located in the middle of four recently developed neighborhoods that are 10 miles from a large metropolitan area. Ten years ago, the area was used for farming; today, new housing or construction exists everywhere. Because most families were transferred by businesses from other parts of the country, the school's ethnic background has changed dramatically. Moreover, Roger Williams's student population has grown dramatically from 270 to 426. Each year, another trailer has been placed alongside the school to accommodate new students. This population increase is putting strain on the school's already extended resources.

A Focus for the Evaluation

The Parent Teachers Organization (PTO) is aware of how the school's resources are being stretched by the recent influx of students and they want to help. Each year, they raise funds for school projects. In the past few years, moneys have been used to purchase new computers for the science lab and other classroom supplies. This year, the PTO wants to give the library additional funds to purchase new books. The PTO's leadership team asked the school's principal, Dr. Lucille Kaney, to meet with them to plan how they might spend the moneys.

Dr. Kaney asked her librarian, Ms. Jane DePietro, and a teacher from each grade level to attend this meeting. She knew the PTO would want her to justify how any funds would be spent; thus an evaluation of library resources would have to be conducted. Evaluations require much time and hard work. Dr. Kaney knew she would have to rely on her staff to conduct the evaluation so she asked for their assistance from the very beginning. Also, because they used the library on a daily basis, she knew her staff would have valuable suggestions about what the library needed. Dr. Kaney viewed her teachers and other staff members as stakeholders who have a strong interest in the quality of the school's programs. (See *Evaluating School Programs: An Educator's Guide,* Chapter 2.) Dr. Kaney knew from previous experiences that the probability of a successful evaluation would be increased if the staff were able to discuss their views and obtain feedback from their colleagues.

Focusing the Evaluation

Dr. Kaney's efforts caused the PTO meeting to go smoothly. The PTO decided to have a fund drive to obtain moneys so that new library books could be purchased. Prior to the actual funds being raised, the PTO requested that the staff determine what types of books or materials were needed. Consequently, amidst the elation of realizing that the library would receive new resources, Dr. Kaney nodded to Ms. DePietro to remind the librarian of the work that needed to be done. Both had served on previous evaluation committees, and each knew the next few months would be busy.

The PTO would raise the money, yet the staff needed to decide which materials should be purchased. Unlike personal decisions, where one could simply buy those books that were most appealing, this decision would involve the systematic collection of information and analysis of needs and resources. One could not simply buy books without conducting an evaluation of the library's resources.

Selecting the Evaluation Team

Several considerations had to be made when setting up the evaluation committee. Dr. Kaney knew that the evaluation's success depended upon her staff's willingness and expertise. Someone was needed to direct the evaluation. Dr. Kaney needed to talk with various people about serving as committee members. Members would be effective if they had the time to participate and were interested in the evaluation topic. Furthermore, committee members had to have knowledge of the content area being evaluated and be willing to learn a bit about program evaluation procedures. Ms. Jane DePietro was asked to be the committee chairperson. She had knowledge of libraries, had some experience with program evaluation, and was respected by her colleagues. Her leadership was necessary for a successful evaluation. Dr. Kaney then asked two teachers from different grade levels to participate. All of the teachers were interested and quite willing to be on the committee. Five parents were asked to participate so that everyone in the school community would be aware of the project's purpose and progress. (See *Evaluating School Programs: An Educator's Guide,* Chapter 2.)

At the first meeting of the evaluation committee, Dr. Kaney thanked each individual for agreeing to serve on the committee and briefly reviewed their responsibilities. Ms. DePietro discussed the steps they would follow and asked each member to talk about what they hoped the committee would establish. Each member brought a different perspective to the committee. Ms. DePietro wanted to make sure that there was a consensus among members about the evaluation's purpose and direction; otherwise, individuals with different expectations could become easily discouraged. Decisions made at this point provided a foundation for the evaluation.

Ms. DePietro helped establish a common starting point by asking members to review a list of standards and indicators of a quality reading and language arts program that was based on recent research. (See Resource B.) The standards and indicators would help the committee create an evaluation focus to determine which resources already existed and which needed to be purchased. Indicator 2.1—"The language arts and reading program provides evidence of a balance of basal reader series, literature, information books, computer-based reading instruction, and/or audiovisual materials"—was selected as the most appropriate indicator on which to focus the evaluation. It became a point of agreement from which the committee could proceed.

Collecting the Information

Even though the evaluation had just begun, much had been accomplished. An evaluation committee had been selected, a focus had been identified, and the first meeting already had been conducted. Indicator 2.1 helped the committee gain a clear sense of what was going to be evaluated. To further clarify the resources that they would be evaluating, Ms. DePietro gave committee members at their next meeting copies of the text, *Through the Eyes of a Child: An Introduction to Children's Literature,* by Donna E. Norton (Columbus, OH: Charles E. Merrill, 1983). The rationale for providing the committee with this book was that, within each major category that Indicator 2.1 listed, the book provided subcategories of texts. For example, within the literature subcategory, there were picture books, traditional literature, modern fantasy, poetry, contemporary realistic fiction, multiethnic literature, and historical fiction. Within the information subcategory, there were books that focused on history and geography, laws of nature, experiments, discoveries, how things worked, hobbies, crafts, how-to books, and biographies. Ms. DePietro explained that a library contained texts from each of these subcategories and that teachers used texts from each subcategory for different purposes. When conducting the evaluation, committee members would have to determine the extent to which the library had texts in each subcategory.

Ms. DePietro sensed that some committee members were a bit overwhelmed by the amount of information that was being presented. To ease their apprehensions, she suggested that they tour the library so they could become familiar with the resources and their locations. First of all, Mrs. DePietro told the parents who were on the committee that the school's basal series were kept in the classrooms. Because they were purchased with district funds, they would not be included in the evaluation. She then showed committee members where different types of literature and information texts were located. While she showed them their locations in the library, she selected examples of each type of literature and information book so that she later could show members the differences between each subcategory. The last area they toured was where the computer and audiovisual materials were kept. Computer equipment included remedial, enrichment, and information software programs whereas audiovisual materials included films and filmstrips. As a result of the tour, committee members were more knowledgeable about the resources they would be evaluating and understood why they had to approach the evaluation in a systematic manner. A book was no longer just a book!

At this point in the evaluation, Ms. DePietro outlined the next task that needed to be addressed. To evaluate the adequacy of the library's resources, the committee would have to identify texts and other library materials as belonging to one of the subcategories. The evaluation would only be successful to the extent that the library holdings were categorized accurately. (See *Evaluating School Programs: An Educator's Guide,* Chapter 3.) Ms. DePietro explained that the committee could take the time to train everyone to identify the various types of books or that groups could be formed in which some members in each group had this knowledge and could share it with others in their group. Because the second option required less time, it was selected. Ms. DePietro told committee members that she would develop a handout that would give descriptions of each type of book. Groups were formed and each group exchanged examples of the genres of books so that everyone would be familiar with how the library materials were to be categorized.

Deciding on an Indicator   The next step was to decide how the needed information (i.e., how many books and other materials were in each of the categories) could be collected. Ms. DePietro had been involved in several program evaluations in her tenure at Roger Williams Elementary School and explained the different ways in which evaluative information could be obtained. She reviewed such strategies as the use of checklists, questionnaires, and interviews and explained how each had certain advantages and disadvantages. A checklist was the committee's only feasible choice because their goal was to evaluate the extent to which the library owned certain types of books and other materials. The committee needed to count the number of different types of books in the library and decide where future purchases were warranted. Questionnaires and interviews were not appropriate because no school personnel would be able to provide the needed information. Once they had categorized and counted the library's holdings, the committee could determine the adequacy of the library's resources by comparing the amount of materials available with the number of students and their curricular needs. Ms. DePietro asked for volunteers to develop a checklist and set a new meeting date for the following week.

Creating a Checklist   The checklist the volunteers developed listed the different categories of texts that were described in the children's literature textbook. Their checklist is shown in Table 1.1. Notice how different resources are listed down the side of the table with subcategories included for each. Along the top of the table is a grade level listing that was consistent with how the library divided its selections.

Ms. DePietro explained that she wanted to have a practice coding session so the committee could work out any inconsistencies in coding. She explained that the committee was to break into two teams of three to four persons and each team was to code 50 books. After coding the 50 books, the committee was to check to see if they consistently coded each book to its appropriate category. During the practice coding, there was a lot of discussion, and committee members frequently referred to the handout they were given. Placing each book into a specific category was not as easy as many had expected. Toward the end of the session, however, most had gained confidence in their abilities to code books accurately. The committee discussed the types of difficulties they experienced and noted how long it took them to code their entries. Based on the amount of time it took, they developed a work schedule for each coding team so that members would know when they were required to participate and how long the coding would take. Before ending the meeting, Ms. DePietro showed the committee where their coding sheets were kept and reminded them to place the completed coding sheets in a locked drawer so that they would be safe. The practice session reinforced the notion that evaluations must be done carefully and systematically.

TABLE 1.1   Checklist for Identifying Library Resources

	Grade Levels	
Library Materials	K-2	3-5
Literature:		
Picture books		
Traditional literature		
Modern fantasy		
Poetry		
Contemporary realistic fiction		
Multiethnic literature		
Historical fiction		
Informational:		
History		
Geography		
Laws of nature		
Experiments		
Discoveries		
How things work		
Hobbies		
Crafts		
How-to books		
Biographies		
Computer-Based Reading:		
Remedial programs		
Enrichment programs		
Informational programs		
Audiovisual:		
Films		
Filmstrips		

Organizing and Analyzing Information

Summarizing the Data

The coding of the library materials was completed in four 3-hour work sessions. Once all materials had been categorized and counted, the committee placed the information from the different sheets on one form. They talked about how the data should be presented. They decided to present the data using the recording categories on the checklist, with percentages shown for each category so the PTO could see where any deficits existed. The results the committee tabulated are presented in Table 1.2. Upon reviewing the information in the table, committee members believed that the data could be understood readily by members of the school community. To make sure, several committee members took examples to show friends to see whether they would have any difficulty understanding and interpreting the table. (See *Evaluating School Programs: An Educator's Guide,* Chapter 4.)

Reporting Information

Interpreting the Data   Now that the data were collected and summarized, the committee still faced the task of interpreting the results. Ms. DePietro showed the committee the American Library Association (ALA) accreditation standards. These standards recommended that libraries were expected to have at least 10 usable books for every student. Given that there were 220 students in Grades K-2 and 225 students in Grades 3-5 at Roger Williams, there should have been 2,200 texts for the younger students and 2,250 texts for the older students—an increase of 1,100 texts for the younger students and 380 texts for the older students. The committee quickly realized that, although the library holdings were adequate 5 years ago, recent enrollment increases placed the library's resources well below the ALA criterion. This conclusion was especially true for K-2 students.

The committee then discussed the school's curricular needs as they related to the school's library resources. For example, there was need for more literature-based texts for Grades K-2, because many of the teachers had adopted a whole-language approach to reading that required numerous books. Furthermore, to address this need, the committee felt the PTO should help the library acquire additional books so that the school would have more traditional literature, modern fantasy, and historical fiction. Furthermore, to address the changing composition of the student body, they felt the school should have more books with a multiethnic flavor. Within the informational text category, the evaluation results suggest that the library needed more books of history, geography, laws of nature, and hobbies.

The committee then examined the resources for Grades 3-5. Given the nature of their homework assignments, teachers believed they should have more informational than literature texts. In particular, based on the evaluation results, there was a need for laws of nature, discoveries, experiments, hobbies, and how-to texts. As with their younger peers, they also needed more multiethnic books.

TABLE 1.2   Number of Library Materials and Percentage Within Category, by Category and Student Grade Level

	Grade Levels			
	K-2		3-5	
Library Materials	(Students = 220)		(Students = 225)	
	Number	Percentage	Number	Percentage
Literature:				
Picture books	75	16	14	2
Traditional literature	123	26	178	25
Modern fantasy	54	12	112	15
Poetry	54	12	49	7
Contemporary realistic fiction	89	19	230	31
Multiethnic literature	46	10	47	7
Historical fiction	25	5	95	13
Subtotal	466		725	
Informational:				
History	15	2	125	11
Geography	23	4	140	12
Laws of nature	48	8	75	7
Experiments	78	12	107	9
Discoveries	96	15	87	8
How things work	98	15	140	12
Hobbies	54	8	84	7
Crafts	78	12	156	14
How-to books	87	14	85	7
Biographies	67	10	146	13
Subtotal	644		1,145	
Total	1,110		1,870	
Computer-Based Reading:				
Remedial programs	45	27	43	26
Enrichment programs	56	34	76	46
Informational programs	65	39	46	28
Total	166		165	
Audiovisual:				
Films	42	48	35	35
Filmstrips	46	52	66	65
Total	88		101	

The only area that still needed to be examined was the computer and audiovisual materials section. Ms. DePietro and the teachers were satisfied with the status of these materials. The difficulty with purchasing these materials, Ms. DePietro explained, was that they were changing so quickly that it was difficult to develop long-term plans. What the school might purchase 2 years from now might not be on the market today. One committee member suggested that perhaps moneys could be set aside to purchase materials as they were needed. This suggestion was adopted by the committee.

Sharing the Information

The final step the committee faced when interpreting their checklist data was to prepare a report. Once a draft report was completed, they would share it with individuals who were not on the committee. The reason for sharing a draft report was that someone might have a different interpretation of the results and should be allowed to voice it. In addition, the committee members might reach different conclusions after they had a chance to think about their work. Ms. DePietro said she would prepare a draft report and provide each committee member with a copy. She asked that each member return any changes to her within a week so that they could be put into a final report for the PTO. (See *Evaluating School Programs: An Educator's Guide,* Chapter 5.)

At a final meeting, Dr. Kaney thanked Ms. DePietro for her direction and the parents and teachers for serving on the committee. The evaluation team shared their findings with other teachers and parents. The PTO already had raised most of the funds and were well ahead of their schedule for raising the remaining moneys. Dr. Kaney mentioned that teachers needed to start thinking about which books they would want in the categories identified by the committee.

Summary of Evaluation Principles

This example illustrated several important principles that should be kept in mind in all evaluations of school programs. As in other vignettes in this guide, we provide a list of these principles. Please refer to *Evaluating School Programs: An Educator's Guide* for a more thorough discussion of evaluation principles.

1. Do not attempt to evaluate every aspect of a program at once. Focus the evaluation by selecting a few indicators of quality from the list in Resource A and use any other appropriate resources. In this vignette, Indicator 2.1 served as a general indicator and subcategories were developed based on a children's literature text.
2. When choosing a method of data collection, try to select an alternative that minimizes the burden on those who will provide information

and can be implemented given your resources and timetable. In this vignette, use of a checklist was straightforward; it involved minimal cost and effort.

3. Whenever possible, collect information in ways that give every member of the group of interest an opportunity to respond. The committee chairperson, Ms. DePietro, made sure everyone voiced their views and asked each committee member as well as stakeholders outside the committee to comment on the draft report. She wanted to make sure that everyone understood and agreed on how the results should be interpreted.

4. When using a checklist, make sure everyone agrees on how to define what is measured and uses the same criteria when applying this definition. Moreover, make sure the data collectors practice coding what is being examined prior to gathering the actual evaluative data. In this example, committee members were given information about how to define different texts and they had an opportunity to practice coding texts.

Cautions Regarding Misinterpretation

The most obvious misinterpretation of these results is to assume that a library has sufficient resources when it obtains a certain number of materials and when texts are purchased according to the curriculum or student body composition. These criteria are important, yet they are not sufficient. Availability of resources should be viewed only as a first step. Materials are beneficial only when students have access to them and when teachers are knowledgeable about their use.

2 Vignette Two

Evaluation of Writing Programs

Where, What, and Why?

Sam Houston Elementary School is located in a poor, rural area of Georgia. It enrolls 667 children in kindergarten through Grade 6, who are bused to Sam Houston from small communities and farms in the surrounding counties. Some families farm or work in small businesses that are supported by the people in the area; many are unemployed. Moreover, because farming is not particularly successful in the area, neither are the businesses. Children are therefore from low-income families that generally have low literacy skills. Sam Houston is, for the most part, racially and socioeconomically homogeneous. About 75% of the school's students are black; the rest are white. Parents want their children to do well in school and support the school's activities as best they can.

Ms. Clara Little, the principal of Sam Houston, is dedicated to the education of the children who attend her school and believes reading and language skills are basic to achievement in other subject areas. She has 28 teachers, 1 media specialist, 2 school counselors, and an instructional leader on her staff. The educational climate of Sam Houston is positive, with teachers and support personnel convinced that the children can succeed in school despite their frequently impoverished backgrounds. Ms. Little works with her teachers and staff to improve the school's effectiveness through a continuing program of selective, focused evaluations. Because of the positive educational climate at

21

Sam Houston, teachers are comfortable with ongoing program evaluation. Certainly, determining what aspect of a school's curriculum needs evaluation is a critical step in school improvement. The systematic collection of data from which to draw conclusions allows schools to determine the strengths and weaknesses of a particular program. With that knowledge, school staff can make informed decisions related to instruction, student achievement, personnel, materials, and other resources (see *Evaluating School Programs: An Educator's Guide,* Chapter 1).

A Focus for the Evaluation

At the end of the previous school year, Ms. Little received complaints from the town's junior high school concerning the writing skills of the students from Sam Houston. She was surprised by the complaints, since 2 years ago her teachers had attended an intensive 2-week summer workshop on writing. Moreover, they had monitored each other's teaching the following year and felt comfortable with the activities and processes they observed.

In the agenda for the beginning-of-the-year faculty meeting that she sent faculty, Ms. Little asked the teachers to think about the complaints she had received. She knew that communication was the key to any successful schoolwide decision, and thus she wanted the teachers to have time to prepare their thoughts about that agenda item. The teachers were stakeholders who had a great interest in the writing program (see *Evaluating School Programs: An Educator's Guide,* Chapter 2).

Focusing the Evaluation

During the meeting, the teachers agreed on a basic premise: that learning to write begins early in a student's journey to literacy, with each year's experiences becoming important pieces of the foundation for the next year's learning. They also agreed that they needed to evaluate the writing component of their language arts program to determine what might contribute to their students' difficulties in junior high school. They then reasoned that, if the students from Sam Houston had weak writing skills when they arrived at junior high school, restricting an evaluation to the year or two prior to the students' entry to junior high school would provide an incomplete picture. On the other hand, evaluating their school's writing program at all levels would provide a more complete picture of children's writing experiences at Sam Houston and, they hoped, would provide insights into the reported problems their students were having at the junior high school. As a result, the teachers proposed that a program evaluation focus on the writing component across the school's K-5 language arts curriculum for the current year.

Ms. Little made sure that the teachers understood that *they* were not being evaluated, that only the school's writing program was being evaluated. She also announced that the evaluation team would have one free afternoon per week to work on the evaluation. She knew the team would need released time to do a good job. The teachers and support staff agreed that an evaluation of the writing program could be useful and helpful to them as they sought to improve the literacy level of their students.

Selecting the Evaluation Team

Ms. Little and the assistant principal, Ms. Smythe, knew that they needed an evaluation team composed of members who were interested in, and somewhat knowledgeable about, evaluation procedures as well as writing (see *Evaluating School Programs: An Educator's Guide,* Chapter 2). They also knew that teachers could learn enough about evaluation to do the job by studying this guide and *Evaluating School Programs: An Educator's Guide* in this series. Fortunately, all of the teachers had attended the composition workshop 2 years earlier, which ensured some knowledge of writing instruction. They decided to ask three teachers who had previously expressed a special interest in writing to help them evaluate the school's writing program. For example, Mr. Bynum, a first-grade teacher, was interested in children's acquisition of writing skills. He also had attended a special institute on the composition process at a regional college that increased his knowledge and interest in writing. Ms. Gillis, an experienced third-grade teacher, did not believe she had children write enough in her class but recognized the need to have children write. She had done some independent reading and had completed a graduate evaluation course. Ms. Hatcher taught sixth grade and wanted to prepare her students for the teachers' expectations at the junior high school they would attend the following year. She had also attended the special institute. All three teachers realized the importance that writing had for their students and were willing to serve on the school's evaluation team, which was to be led by Ms. Smythe.

Deciding on an Indicator

A reading and language arts curriculum is complex, interrelated, and multifaceted because language arts programs include reading, writing, listening, and speaking, with each area having a number of components. Ms. Little suggested that the teachers and Ms. Smythe review the problem that prompted the evaluation, namely, the poor writing performances of their students when they entered junior high school, and then review the list of quality reading and language arts standards and indicators provided in Resource A of this guide to help them decide where to start.

After considering the list of standards and indicators, the evaluation team realized that there were many indicators of a quality writing program. They also concluded that evaluating many of the indicators could be unproductive if teachers were not allowing time in their schedules for writing and writing instruction. Thus the evaluation team decided that, although writing was included in their program goals and they had had special preparation in writing, it was important to determine whether their program included adequate writing instruction and opportunities for students to write. In other words, the evaluation team wanted to look at the amount of time scheduled for writing instruction and actual writing because they believed the quality of instruction, based on prior observations, was adequate. It might be that students' opportunities for and instruction in writing were quite good but there were just not enough of them. Consequently, they selected Indicator 13.1—"The language arts and reading program provides evidence of the allotment of substantial time to writing"—as the point at which to begin their evaluation. Ms. Little agreed that satisfaction of this indicator seemed to be prerequisite to the other writing indicators, given the teachers' writing background. In fact, perceived deficiencies related to this indicator might need to be addressed before additional writing indicators could be evaluated.

Collecting Information

Defining the Terms Used in the Selected Indicator

The evaluation team began by seeking answers to certain questions. What exactly did the terms in the indicator mean? How could the program's status on the indicator be evaluated? What constraints should they consider as they developed their evaluation plan? How long would the evaluation need to take to give a fair representation of what was happening in the writing program? How could they use the results of the evaluation to strengthen Sam Houston's writing program? (See *Evaluating School Programs: An Educator's Guide,* Chapter 3.)

As the team began to implement Indicator 13.1, they admitted to some confusion. It was apparent that three notions needed to be clarified before settling on an assessment strategy. First, the notion of "writing" had to be defined. The team determined that their definition of "writing" should be broad enough to include both instruction to prepare students for composing and the actual composing of continuous text. For example, composition or writing instruction would include time spent teaching children to respond to writing assignments, plan the content and structure of a composition, draft, revise, and/or edit their papers. Conversely, they agreed that selecting words to write on a blank line in a sentence, copying information from the chalkboard, penmanship practice, or writing sentences using spelling or vocabulary words did not constitute composing.

Second, "allotment of substantial time to writing" needed to be implemented. The team decided that "substantial time" would be expressed as a percentage of the time scheduled for all language arts, specifically reading, writing, spelling, listening, and speaking activities. Ms. Little had asked teachers to spend a total of 120 minutes a day or 600 minutes a week (2 hours a day or 10 hours a week) on language arts. After checking several reading-language arts reference books, the team found no recommended percentage of time for writing instruction; however, they decided that a reasonable and substantial amount of the time spent on writing would be 30% of the time the school required for language arts. This amounted to only 36 minutes a day or 2 hours a week spent on writing, but the team knew that teachers had to use the remaining instructional time to address the other components of the language arts. They further acknowledged that, because the components of language arts were so closely interrelated, instruction in those components would never be mutually exclusive. That is, writing time would, of necessity, include spelling practice; time spent reading might require written responses; and so on.

Third, "allotment of substantial time" needed to be defined. To secure results that would be interpretable, it was important to measure the same characteristic in each class. (See *Evaluating School Programs: An Educator's Guide,* Chapter 3.) The team decided that "allotted time" meant the actual time that a teacher allocated to writing but did not mean that students were, necessarily, actively engaged in academic instruction. That is, allotted time simply meant the time the teacher provided for student writing or writing instruction regardless of whether the students participated in writing during that time. For example, Bobby's teacher might schedule 30 minutes per day for free writing (allotted time), but Bobby might be drawing airplanes rather than actually writing (academic engaged time).

Choosing the Information Source

The evaluation team then considered several ways to assess Indicator 13.1, which clearly required some measurement of time allotted for writing. For example, the team considered interviews with a few teachers at the end of each day to ask about that day's class time spent writing; however, they rejected interviews for three reasons. First, interviewing a few teachers would not give a fair picture of the entire school. Second, teachers might not be interested or willing to be interviewed each day after school because they would be tired after a long day in the classroom. Third, even though the results of the interviews would be kept confidential, interviews aren't anonymous (teachers might be reluctant to be acknowledge that they hadn't spent much class time on writing).

Classroom observations that recorded time spent writing were also considered, but, given the expense of classroom observations (in time and money), the evaluation team discarded observations as an option. Finally, the team decided to ask the teachers to keep a daily log for 3 weeks. The teachers would record the beginning time and ending time of the day's writing instruction, acknowledging that the log would reflect some days with no writing activities. One problem with the notion of a log was the potential inaccuracy of self-reporting. People simply want to look good. Teachers might make a special effort to schedule writing instruction because they knew their logs would be reviewed, or, inadvertently, they might tend to overreport time spent on writing instruction. The evaluation team hoped, however, that collecting data over a 3-week period would make the information more trustworthy by acclimating teachers to the reporting task.

The evaluation team explained their plan to Ms. Little, who checked with the staff at the next faculty meeting. She wanted to make sure that there were no objections to the evaluation team's proposal to use a daily time log. Ms. Little explained why the evaluation team selected Indicator 13.1 and its importance. She then discussed the measurement strategies the team considered before deciding on a time log. Finally, she urged the teachers not to make any modifications to their writing instruction time or procedures during the subsequent weeks so that the data collected would validly indicate their typical behavior.

The members of the evaluation team looked in several program evaluation books for a time log that would meet their needs and also in a textbook on writing instruction. Although they were unable to find what they were looking for, their study of other time logs enabled them to design a form that met their needs. They were pleased to notice that they had already addressed some of the cautions concerning time logs. For instance, they had operationally defined the terms in Indicator 13.1. They knew how long they wanted the data collection period to last and what their source of data was to be. The evaluation team believed that securing data from a representative sample of teachers would be necessary because they wanted to be able to draw conclusions about the time allotted to writing by all teachers in the school. They had thought that they would just randomly sample 28 teachers' time logs rather than collect data from all of the teachers. The program evaluation books, however, recommended collecting information from everyone if the group being sampled was smaller than 100. It is difficult to obtain a representative sample when the group being sampled is small (see *Evaluating School Programs: An Educator's Guide,* Chapter 3). As a result of this recommendation, Ms. Smythe suggested that it would be time consuming, but far wiser, to collect data anonymously from every teacher.

Creating the Time Log   The team created the following time log and decided to pilot test it in their own classrooms. They wanted to see if it was workable and how long it would take teachers to complete each day's entry. If the task was too time consuming, they would have to rethink their evaluation decision. As it turned out, the teachers on the evaluation team found they could very easily and quickly complete the log each day; consequently, they decided to go ahead with their plan. They briefed the faculty on the use of the log. The faculty agreed to record their writing instruction time as accurately as they reasonably could to expedite the evaluation team's task.

They also agreed the logs would be anonymous but would have a responding teacher's grade level noted. Some of the teachers asked Ms. Little if the evaluation team could compute the percentage of time spent on writing for their individual classes because they were interested in learning about their own teaching. Ms. Little agreed to ask the evaluation team to complete those computations if a teacher requested them but suggested the teachers keep a duplicate log so that the one the team used for the schoolwide data analysis remained anonymous (see *Evaluating School Programs: An Educator's Guide,* Chapter 3).

Organizing and Analyzing Information

The team decided that Ms. Smythe, Mr. Bynum, Ms. Gillis, and Ms. Hatcher would each analyze data from the time logs of seven teachers. In addition, Ms. Smythe would analyze data for the whole school (all teachers, taken together) because her school day was more flexible than the teachers' day. Time spent on writing would be recorded in minutes. After practicing, members of the evaluation team determined they could analyze data from a log in about 5 minutes. Team members thus spent about 35 to 45 minutes each for the initial computations. The time log is presented in Table 2.1.

Summarizing the Data   After 3 weeks, the evaluation team summarized their data. They decided that, to compute the percentage of the recommended language arts time the entire school allotted to writing, they needed to sum the reported time spent on writing for the 3-week period across individual teachers and divide that total by the school's 3-week recommended time for language arts. Thus they first multiplied Ms. Little's recommended weekly language arts time to get a 3-week recommended language arts time (600 minutes × 3 = 1,800 minutes). Next, they multiplied the 3-week recommended language arts time by the number of teachers to get the school's 3-week recommended language arts time (1,800 minutes × 28 teachers = 50,400 minutes).

TABLE 2.1   Time Log for Time Allotted for Writing

Grade level _____

Please record the beginning and ending time (to the nearest minute) that you spend on writing instruction. Remember that, for this log, "writing instruction" is considered time spent on instruction that leads to students' composing continuous text or time students spend actually composing continuous text.

Time	Monday	Tuesday	Wednesday	Thursday	Friday
Week 1					
begin					
end					
begin					
end					
begin					
end					
Daily Totals					
(Office use only)					
Weekly Total					
(Office use only)					
Week 2					
begin					
end					
begin					
end					
begin					
end					
Daily Totals					
(Office use only)					
Weekly Total					
(Office use only)					
Week 3					
begin					
end					
begin					
end					
begin					
end					
Grand Total					
(Office use only)					

Then the team totaled the teachers' time logs to arrive at the school's actual time spent on writing. See Table 2.2 for the results.

Finally, they divided the school's actual time spent on writing by the schoolwide recommended time for language arts instruction and

TABLE 2.2   Results From the Evaluation of Time Allotted for Writing

Teacher Level	Minutes
Kindergarten Teachers	
Teacher 1	400
Teacher 2	535
Teacher 3	600
Teacher 4	490
First-Grade Teachers	
Teacher 5	395
Teacher 6	470
Teacher 7	560
Teacher 8	530
Second-Grade Teachers	
Teacher 9	510
Teacher 10	530
Teacher 11	580
Teacher 12	595
Third-Grade Teachers	
Teacher 13	275
Teacher 14	480
Teacher 15	200
Teacher 16	570
Fourth-Grade Teachers	
Teacher 17	250
Teacher 18	300
Teacher 19	315
Teacher 20	285
Fifth-Grade Teachers	
Teacher 21	270
Teacher 22	200
Teacher 23	310
Teacher 24	150
Sixth-Grade Teachers	
Teacher 25	240
Teacher 26	200
Teacher 27	315
Teacher 28	170
Total actual time spent writing	10,725

multiplied that ratio by 100. This gave the team the percentage of recommended language arts time the teachers at the Sam Houston

TABLE 2.3   Results From the Evaluation of the Percentage of Recommended Language Arts Instructional Time Allocated to Writing, by Grade Level

Grade Level	Percentage of Writing Time
Kindergarten	28
First Grade	27
Second Grade	31
Third Grade	21
Fourth Grade	16
Fifth Grade	13
Sixth Grade	13

Elementary School spent on writing during the target time period (10,725 minutes/50,400 minutes = .21 or 21%).

Reporting Information

Comparing Responses by Grade Level   Ms. Smythe was aware that stakeholders should be kept informed about the evaluation activities and the progress the evaluation team was making (see *Evaluating School Programs: An Educator's Guide,* Chapter 5). In this case, the evaluation team found their results interesting but initially only shared their findings with Ms. Little. As she considered the 21% of recommended language arts instruction time with the school's actual writing instruction time, Ms. Little believed that the figure did not fairly represent what she knew was going on in the kindergarten, first, and second grades. She believed that the percentage should be computed by grade levels if results were to be useful to the teachers and the school. The evaluation team then calculated the percentage of time teachers spent on writing for each grade level. They divided the actual time spent on writing at each grade level by the 3-week recommended language arts time. It was important for the team to remember that they had to recompute the 3-week recommended language arts time by multiplying the recommended time by the number of teachers at each grade level (1,800 minutes × 4 teachers = 7,200 minutes). The evaluation team then gave Ms. Little the additional data she requested. (See Table 2.3 for results.)

Sharing the Information   In the spirit of improving the school's performance, and thereby improving the writing program, Ms. Little arranged a meeting with the teachers to discuss the results of the evaluation and to develop an improvement strategy (see *Evaluating School Programs: An Educator's Guide,* Chapter 5). Emphasizing the positive findings of the evaluation, Ms. Little noted that every teacher was scheduling some instructional time for writing. The results of the evaluation, however, indicated a clear need to increase the classroom time allotted to writing in most grades, but particularly in the intermediate grades.

Ms. Little set up a schedule for discussions with teachers at each grade level to discover why they did not allot more class time to writing. During those discussions, the upper-grade teachers indicated that they were willing to schedule more class time for writing but confessed that, despite the summer writing workshop they had attended, they did not know how to use additional time effectively. They pointed out that the workshop clearly had been designed for teachers at the primary grades.

Ms. Little obtained financial support from the school district's staff development fund. She believed that one-shot inservice workshops were not often effective and that ongoing meetings were more likely to produce change. She wanted to help teachers develop the knowledge to feel comfortable increasing class time for writing and the competence to use that time wisely.

Finally, Ms. Little worked with the area university to schedule a graduate course on writing instruction to be taught after school one afternoon a week. The instructor agreed to offer the course at Sam Houston so that all of the teachers could attend conveniently.

Summary of Evaluation Principles

This example illustrated several important principles that should be kept in mind in all evaluations of school programs. As in other examples in this guide, we provide a list of these principles:

1. Do not attempt to evaluate every aspect of a program at once. Focus the evaluation by selecting a few indicators of quality from the list in Resource A. In this case, the evaluation team considered the teachers' past experiences with writing workshops and their own classroom observations to help them focus on *time* allocated to writing instruction, which they believed to be prerequisite to selecting writing indicators that evaluated other aspects of a writing program.

2. When choosing a method of data collection, try to select an alternative that minimizes the burden on those who will be asked to provide information. At Ms. Little's school, the evaluation team selected a time log because they wanted to assess time allotted to writing. They pilot tested the log in their own classrooms to assure themselves it was not inordinately time consuming to fill out.

3. Remember that evaluation often requires hard judgments and negative responses that people might be reluctant to express. If at all possible, design the evaluation in ways that permit those who provide information to preserve their privacy. Always guarantee confidentiality. If possible, provide anonymity. In this scenario, the

teachers remained anonymous although they did have to indicate their grade level. Teachers who wanted an analysis of their own scheduled writing instruction were willing to forgo their anonymity.

4. Whenever possible, collect information in ways that give every member of the group of interest an opportunity to respond. Remember that you typically will want to draw conclusions about the judgments of "all teachers," "all administrators," or "all students in Grade X." When the group to be represented is small (say, fewer than 100), collecting information from everyone is better than collecting information from a sample. It is difficult to obtain a representative sample when the group to be sampled is small. In this case, the entire faculty completed the time log so that the evaluation team could draw conclusions about the activities of all the teachers.

5. Ask questions your information providers are able to answer, and avoid questions that require speculation. Remember that behaviors can be observed, but judgments concerning knowledge are speculative. A time log was easily completed and required no judgments that were speculative.

6. Collect information that will help to identify areas of program success and weakness and guide remedial actions when improvement is needed. The information provided by the time log identified particular grade levels that needed help. Follow-up discussions guided the remedial actions that were needed.

7. Whenever possible, seek redundant information. Ask several questions about each important evaluation issue, and seek information from more than one source. Consistent information from several sources is more trustworthy than information from a single source. Consistent responses to several questions are far more trustworthy than responses to a single question. In this case, information was collected across 3 weeks from all teachers in all grade levels (several sources).

Alternatives to the Strategy Used Here

Other Sources for and Methods of Collecting Information

Because Indicator 13.1 was phrased in terms of allotted time, actual scheduled time was the obvious source of information for assessing this indicator. As discussed earlier, the evaluation team considered and rejected the possibilities of collecting information about time allotted to writing from teachers through face-to-face interviews or observations. The evaluation team might have gained additional insights, however, by using interviews after the teachers had completed their anonymous time logs. Interviews have the advantage of permitting in-depth probing and clarification of initial information, whereas time logs or observation do not. In this evaluation, Ms. Little used follow-up discussions with teachers in each grade to obtain information on the reasons the intermediate-grade teachers did not schedule sufficient time for writing. Keep in mind that the objective of this evaluation was securing information about the time allotted to writing instruction so that the writing program could be improved.

Cautions Regarding Misinterpretation

Limitations of the Instrument

It would be easy to summarize the results of this evaluation by concluding that Sam Houston Elementary School was not scheduling an adequate amount of time for writing instruction or to conclude that the intermediate-grade teachers were primarily responsible for the students' poor showing at the junior high school. Certainly, such a summary is certainly too glib given the data (see *Evaluating School Programs: An Educator's Guide,* Chapter 5).

It is true that the primary teachers seemed far more likely to schedule class time for writing instruction than the intermediate-grade teachers and that the intermediate-grade teachers appeared to need to make scheduling changes in their lesson plans. Information supporting these conclusions was, however, collected with one instrument during one 3-week period. The findings might have differed had the data been collected 2 months earlier or later.

It is also very important to remember that this evaluation did not touch on what occurred during the scheduled time or on the quality of those events. This evaluation sought data on teachers' scheduled time for writing instruction. A shorter time that is well planned may be more effective than a longer time during which children are off task or are involved in inappropriate activities. The next logical step for the evaluation team is to consider the events that occur during time scheduled for writing instruction and the quality of those events.

3

Vignette Three

Evaluation of Listening-Speaking Programs

Where, What, and Why?

Located in an upper-middle-class suburb of a large metropolitan area, the Jimmy Carter Middle School was built in the late 1970s to accommodate a rapidly expanding city. It enrolls 986 students whose well-educated parents are actively involved with the school through the PTO and a parents' volunteer tutoring group. About 90% of the school's students are white; the rest are black, Oriental, or southeast Asian. Carter Middle is not particularly racially diverse or socioeconomically diverse; on the contrary, it has a mostly homogeneous student body.

May Worthington, the principal of Carter Middle, works with a staff of 40 teachers, 1 vice principal, 1 school counselor, 2 reading specialists, and 1 media specialist. In her 12 years as principal, she has seen her school's enrollment and staff initially grow rapidly but stabilize about 5 years ago. Ms. Worthington is proud of the accomplishments of her faculty, who, she believes, are thoughtful, creative professionals committed to high quality education.

Because Carter Middle's teachers see Ms. Worthington as fair and supportive, they are willing to participate in ongoing program evaluation. The instructional program is therefore continually being improved through an ongoing program of selective, focused evaluations. The teachers and staff realize that sound program evaluations have a number of payoffs for students, educators, and the general public (see *Evaluating School Programs: An Educator's Guide,* Chapter 2). Certainly a critical first step is determining what aspect of a curriculum needs evaluation. Once that decision is made, then the systematic gathering of data from which to draw conclusions allows the school to determine the strengths and weaknesses of the particular program being evaluated. With that knowledge, the school can make informed decisions related to instruction, student achievement, personnel, materials, and other resources.

A Focus for the Evaluation

Focusing the Evaluation   In August, at the first faculty meeting for professional educators employed by Carter Middle School, the teachers, as stakeholders interested in the quality of their curriculum, discussed their concerns about the school's reading and language arts curriculum. They subsequently agreed that the schoolwide evaluation focus for the current year would be the reading and language arts program with its complex and interrelated curriculum. The teachers were specifically concerned with the listening and speaking aspects of the reading and language arts program, because they suspected those components of the program might be neglected in their school. Although the teachers' stated curricular objective was to provide effective listening and speaking instruction as well as adequate listening and speaking opportunities for students, they were not sure the objective was being met. To determine if the listening and speaking aspect of their language arts program needed improvement, they needed to find out where program strengths and weaknesses were. They knew that a program evaluation that focused on the listening and speaking aspects of language arts could provide a basis for change or modification of the program. Evaluating even a small part of a program takes time and money, however, both of which were in short supply at Carter Middle School (see *Evaluating School Programs: An Educator's Guide,* Chapter 2).

Selecting the Evaluation Team   Ms. Worthington was aware that an evaluation team needed members who were interested and somewhat knowledgeable about evaluation as well as the content of the program. She also knew that she had to arrange time for the team members to conduct the evaluation. For a variety of reasons, three Carter teachers indicated an interest in working with Ms. Worthington to evaluate the listening and speaking aspect of the school's reading and language arts program. Ms. Homan, a seventh-grade social studies teacher, depended on the students in her classroom to develop listening and speaking skills without much instruction from her; however, she realized that she was probably not as effective in this area as she could be. A sound program evaluation could ultimately help her improve and provide additional listening and speaking opportunities for her students. Ms. Hines believed drama activities were important for her overactive eighth graders and wanted an opportunity to learn more about how drama activities were embedded within the listening and speaking components of a reading and language arts program. Mr. Neville, in his second year of teaching sixth-grade reading, relied on the basal series to help him determine when to schedule listening and speaking activities appropriate to his pupils' different developmental levels. He was concerned that the teacher's manual for the basal series was not offering enough guidance in listening and speaking instruction for him to do an effective job. All three teachers recognized the value of an effective listening and speaking component in the school's program and were willing to devote a little extra time if it could be made more effective.

To learn more about listening and speaking goals of reading-language arts curricula so that they could make informed decisions for the evaluation, the teachers and Ms. Worthington reviewed language arts textbooks, pertinent journal articles in *Language Arts* and *The Reading Teacher* (journals published by the National Council of Teachers of English [NCTE] and the International Reading Association [IRA], respectively), and other publications by the NCTE and IRA, which helped them learn the current thinking of experts in the field. They also studied the list of standards and indicators of quality reading-language arts programs provided in Resource A of this guide and based on educational research findings.

Selecting Indicators to Evaluate

After several discussions, they selected Standard 18, which stated: "A high quality language arts and reading curriculum includes instruction in speaking and listening skills for comprehensive, critical, and appreciative listening comprehension as well as formal and informal speaking opportunities." The committee noticed that six indicators were subsumed under this standard. They discussed the meanings of the indicators for this standard and quickly realized they would have to restrict their data collection primarily to no more than three indicators. To collect data for all six indicators would be beyond the scope of their focus as well as their time. Indicators 18.2, 18.4, and 18.6 seemed to hold the most promise for their task. Indicator 18.2 stated, "The language arts and reading program shows evidence of the provision of instruction in detecting propaganda and persuasive language." Indicator 18.4 stated, "The language arts and reading program shows evidence of instruction in preparing oral reports, particularly in gathering and organizing information." And Indicator 18.6 suggested, "The language arts and reading program shows evidence that students have had a variety of opportunities to engage in informative language activities, such as conversations, dialogues, and classroom interviewing." The committee agreed that these three indicators reflected the faculty concerns about student opportunities to develop listening and speaking skills through instruction or actual language activities.

Thus Indicators 18.2, 18.4, and 18.6 became the targets of their data collection and the point at which they began their evaluation. Perceived deficiencies in any of these areas would alert the faculty that listening and speaking curricular improvements probably needed to be made. The committee also believed these indicators were so closely related that they would be able to gather data on each indicator at one time. Furthermore, Ms. Worthington suggested that other components of the reading and language arts program with which they were concerned could be evaluated either later in the school year or during the following school year.

Collecting Information

Choosing a Data Collection Instrument

The evaluation team considered several ways to assess Indicators 18.2, 18.4, and 18.6, such as interviews, discussions, observation checklists, surveys, and questionnaires. (See *Evaluating School Programs: An Educator's Guide,* Chapter 3.) It was clear from the wording of the indicators that they had to determine the speaking and listening opportunities they and their fellow teachers provided students. For example, they considered interviewing a few teachers right after school as one possibility but rejected the idea because they realized that the responses of a few teachers might not reflect the responses of all teachers at Carter Middle School. Also, interviews conducted right after school had several drawbacks. The time might be inconvenient for some teachers. After a long day in the classroom, teachers would be tired, not much interested in being interviewed, or have difficulty accurately recalling what actually happened in their classrooms. Although the results of interviews can be kept confidential, interviews aren't anonymous, so teachers might be reluctant to express their views of the listening and speaking program freely.

Holding a meeting of all teachers to discuss the quality of the listening-speaking program was rejected for many of the same reasons, as well as some others. Finding a convenient time for everyone would be difficult. A meeting during the school day would take teachers out of their classrooms, and a meeting after school would catch teachers when they were tired. In addition, some teachers might be reluctant to speak up in a meeting, and others might dominate the discussion so that only the views of a few should be heard. There would be no guarantee that the views of the few would reflect the views of all teachers.

The group also considered classroom observations, believing observations to be the most accurate way to assess what speaking and listening opportunities were available for students. Unfortunately, arranging observations is a costly effort in time and resources. For those reasons, the team rejected classroom observations to measure the indicators.

After rejecting these alternatives, the team settled on the idea of sending a questionnaire to all 37 Carter teachers who weren't on the evaluation team and the 2 reading specialists, in addition to completing the questionnaire themselves. This approach had several advantages compared with the rejected alternatives. Teachers would feel free to express their views freely on an anonymous questionnaire. Judgments could be collected from all teachers at Carter Middle School, not just a few. Teachers could complete the questionnaire at a time of their own choosing, making the response task more convenient.

Designing the Questionnaire

The four members of the evaluation team tried to find an example of a questionnaire that they could use to assess Indicators 18.2, 18.4, and 18.6. They searched several textbooks on school program evaluation as well as a book on the design of reading-language arts programs. None of these books had exactly what they were looking for, but one of the program evaluation books did contain a questionnaire that seemed to be in a useful format. Using a "Likert scale," the questionnaire had a list of statements about the program being evaluated—some positive statements and some negative—each followed by a 5-point scale that read: "strongly disagree," "disagree somewhat," "uncertain," "agree somewhat," and "strongly agree."

The book explained that some items should be stated negatively because it had been found that people tend to agree with a long list containing only positive statements, just out of habit. This tendency to agree with positive statements was called a "response set." "Response sets" occur when all items in a questionnaire have the same structure or format. According to the book, a major source of invalid results involving the use of Likert scales are questionnaires that encourage a "response set," but this problem could be avoided easily by using a mixture of positive and negative statements. The evaluation team decided to adopt this format and to add a statement at the end inviting the teachers to provide any additional comments they chose concerning the overall quality of the school's listening and speaking components of the reading and language arts program.

The questionnaire contained at least one statement that was designed to assess each of Indicators 18.2, 18.4, and 18.6. Recall that Indicator 18.2 concerned "evidence of the provision of instruction in detecting propaganda and persuasive language." Statements 1, 7, and 9 in the questionnaire were intended to indicate teachers' perceptions about the instruction the school provided students related to propaganda and persuasive language. Indicator 18.4 involved "evidence of instruction in preparing oral reports, particularly in gathering and organizing information." Statements 3, 5, 8, and 10 were related to the effectiveness of instruction for students' preparation and presentation of oral reports. Indicator 18.6 focused on "evidence that students have had a variety of opportunities to engage in informative language activities, such as conversations, dialogues, and classroom interviewing." Statements 2, 4, and 6 were designed to indicate teachers' perceptions about informative language activities provided for students. By design, the evaluation team constructed more statements pertaining to Indicator 18.4 than to Indicators 18.2 or 18.6. They recognized that the latter indicators were somewhat narrower in design than Indicator 18.4. They considered gathering and organizing information to be basic to listening and speaking effectively; consequently, they wanted more opportunities to gather information on Indicator 18.4 than they planned to create to gather data on Indicators 18.2 or 18.6. Their final questionnaire is presented in Table 3.1.

At the next regularly scheduled staff meeting, Ms. Worthington asked Ms. Homan to explain what the evaluation team recommended. She also secured the agreement of all Carter teachers to complete the questionnaire and return it to Ms. Homan within a week of receiving it. Teachers were to call any member of the evaluation team for clarification if they had any questions about the content of the questionnaire. Questionnaires would be distributed to teachers in large manila envelopes by placing them in the teachers' mailboxes outside Ms. Worthington's office.

Organizing and Analyzing the Information

By November 20, each teacher, including the three teachers on the evaluation team, had left a completed questionnaire in Ms. Homan's mailbox. Ms. Homan, Ms. Hines, and Mr. Neville worked together to summarize the teachers' questionnaire responses so they could be interpreted. They began by counting the number of responses to each option after each of the 10 statements and, then, to make the results easier to understand, they calculated the percentage of the teachers who chose each response. For example, for Statement 1, the numbers of teachers who selected each response were as follows: SD = 4, DS = 31, U = 4, AS = 3, and SA = 0.

Organizing the Data   These results indicated that 4 of the teachers "strongly disagreed" (SD) with the statement, 31 "disagreed somewhat" (DS) with the statement, 4 were "uncertain" (U) about their response to the statement, 3 "agreed somewhat" (AS) with the statement, and none "strongly agreed" (SA) with the statement. Each of these response counts was converted to a percentage by first dividing it by the total number of

TABLE 3.1   Listening-Speaking Program Evaluation Questionnaire

CARTER MIDDLE SCHOOL LISTENING-SPEAKING PROGRAM EVALUATION QUESTIONNAIRE

Directions: Please mark the one column after each of the following statements that best describes your own judgment about the statement. Put a check mark in the "SA" column if you "strongly agree" with the statement; mark the "AS" column if you "agree somewhat" with the statement; mark the "U" column if you are "uncertain" about the statement; mark the "DS" column if you "disagree somewhat" with the statement; and mark the "SD" column if you "strongly disagree" with the statement. Be certain that you have expressed your judgment for each of the 10 statements.

Use the space below Statement 10 to write any comments you have about the overall quality of our school's listening-speaking program or any suggestions for improving the program. Add as many pages as you need to express your comments and suggestions. Do not put your name anywhere on the questionnaire or on any pages you add. Place your completed questionnaire inside the large envelope and place it in Ms. Homan's mailbox no later than November 20.

1. Students receive adequate instruction in detecting propaganda techniques as they listen to speakers on television, on the radio, or in person.
   SD   DS   U   AS   SA

2. Students often receive opportunities to discuss topics cooperatively during class time.
   SD   DS   U   AS   SA

3. Students receive little instruction to help them locate and gather pertinent information needed for oral reports.
   SD   DS   U   AS   SA

4. Students rarely work together to plan and conduct interviews with classmates, faculty, or other adults with special expertise.
   SD   DS   U   AS   SA

5. Students usually receive adequate instruction that enables them to present well-organized oral reports.
   SD   DS   U   AS   SA

6. Students rarely have opportunities to participate in dialogues about topics being studied with their classmates.
   SD   DS   U   AS   SA

7. Students rarely receive instructions to help them recognize the persuasive language speakers use to sway audiences.
   SD   DS   U   AS   SA

8. Students have difficulty organizing information to present orally to their classmates because they receive little instruction in how to organize information.
   SD   DS   U   AS   SA

9. Students are instructed in and thus able to use propaganda effectively when speaking persuasively to the class.
   SD   DS   U   AS   SA

10. Students are effective when they are asked to organize information and report orally to an audience as a result of effective instruction.
   SD   DS   U   AS   SA

Please use the space below to add any comments or suggestions you'd like to make concerning the overall quality of the listening-speaking program at Carter Middle School, the strengths and weaknesses of the program, and how the program should be improved. Attach additional pages if needed.

teachers surveyed (42) and then multiplying the resulting fraction by 100. The percentages were rounded to whole numbers to simplify the task of interpretation. For example, the percentage of teachers who "disagreed somewhat" with Statement 1 was found to be $(31/42) \times 100 = (0.738) \times (100) = 73.8\%$, which is rounded up to 74%. The results of the responses to each statement analyzed in this way are shown in Table 3.2.

Interpreting the Data

Because 84% of the teachers marked "strongly disagree/disagree somewhat" in response to Statement 1, "Students receive adequate instruction in detecting propaganda techniques . . ."; 83% of the teachers marked "strongly agree/agree somewhat" to Statement 7, "Students rarely receive instruction to help them recognize the persuasive language speakers use . . ."; and 62% of the teachers marked "strongly disagree/disagree somewhat" to Statement 9, "Students are instructed and thus able to use propaganda effectively when speaking persuasively . . .," the evaluation team concluded that the components of the listening-speaking program that addressed propaganda and persuasive language were being implemented inadequately.

The teachers' responses to Indicator 18.4 (Statements 3, 5, 8, and 10) were not so clear. Their responses were mixed to Statement 3, which asked about instruction that students receive to help them to locate and gather pertinent information for oral reports. That is, some teachers agreed that students received little instruction to help them to locate and gather information (27% and 28%) but others (18% and 10%) disagreed that students lacked that instruction. On the other hand, the teachers clearly indicated on Statements 5, 8, and 10 that they do not think students receive enough instruction to enable them to present well-organized oral reports to an audience. In other words, according to the teachers, students may be able to *find* the pertinent information for their oral reports, but *organizing* and *presenting* that information appeared to be troublesome for them.

Finally, the survey responses to Statements 2, 4, and 6, which were related to Indicator 18.6, were mixed. Whether the statement was negatively or positively worded, the teachers did not clearly agree about opportunities for student discussions. The 31% and 38% of the teachers who marked "strongly agree" or "agree somewhat" in response to Statement 2, "Students often receive opportunities to discuss topics cooperatively during class time," conflicts somewhat with the 35% "uncertain" responses to Statement 4, "Students rarely work together to plan and conduct interviews with classmates, faculty, or other adults with special expertise." A further indication that perceptions for Indicator 18.6 are mixed was the results from Statement 6 that pertained to opportunities to participate in dialogues. Responses to Statement 6 indicate 32% of the teachers agree that students do work together on

TABLE 3.2   Listening-Speaking Program Evaluation Results

1. Students receive adequate instruction in detecting propaganda techniques as they listen to speakers on television, on the radio, or in person.

SD	DS	U	AS	SA
10%	74%	10%	6%	0%

2. Students often receive opportunities to discuss topics cooperatively during class time.

SD	DS	U	AS	SA
0%	12%	19%	38%	31%

3. Students receive little instruction to help them locate and gather pertinent information needed for oral reports.

SD	DS	U	AS	SA
18%	10%	17%	27%	28%

4. Students rarely work together to plan and conduct interviews with classmates, faculty, or other adults with special expertise.

SD	DS	U	AS	SA
10%	41%	35%	10%	4%

5. Students usually receive adequate instruction that enables them to present well-organized oral reports.

SD	DS	U	AS	SA
45%	43%	6%	6%	0%

6. Students rarely have opportunities to participate in dialogues with their classmates about current topics.

SD	DS	U	AS	SA
13%	19%	36%	18%	14%

7. Students rarely receive instruction to help them recognize the persuasive language speakers use to sway audiences.

SD	DS	U	AS	SA
5%	6%	6%	16%	67%

8. Students have difficulty organizing information to present orally to their classmates because they receive little instruction in how to organize information.

SD	DS	U	AS	SA
0%	9%	13%	22%	56%

9. Students are instructed in and thus able to use propaganda effectively when speaking persuasively to the class.

SD	DS	U	AS	SA
30%	32%	24%	12%	2%

10. Students are effective when they are asked to organize information and report orally to an audience as a result of effective instruction.

SD	DS	U	AS	SA
37%	46%	9%	8%	0%

problem-solving tasks, 32% do not agree, and 35% are uncertain. These responses indicate less than unanimous agreement.

Reporting Information

Sharing the Information

In the spirit of improving the listening and speaking aspects of the reading and language arts program, Ms. Worthington provided the faculty with the results of the questionnaire and arranged a later meeting with the teachers to discuss the results of the survey (see *Evaluating School Programs: An Educator's Guide,* Chapter 5). She wanted the faculty to have time to reflect on the survey results. She also wanted time to develop an improvement strategy consistent with the evaluation results. When the meeting occurred, Ms. Worthington emphasized the positive findings of the survey first, pointing out that results indicated that the teachers believed students could locate pertinent information for their oral reports.

The survey results, however, suggested a clear instructional need to increase the students' ability to organize the information they locate and present that information orally to an audience. The other areas of great need seemed to be helping students recognize propaganda and persuasive language when they hear it as well as providing opportunities for students to engage in language activities such as interviews, dialogues, and conversations. In sum, based on the results of the questionnaire, the listening and speaking components of the reading and language arts programs at Carter Middle School appeared to need attention from the teachers.

Making Decisions Based on the Information

To help the teachers develop new skills in these areas, Ms. Worthington obtained financial support from the school district's staff development fund for an outside consultant to provide a series of four workshops on discussion techniques. She also worked with the local university to offer a communication course that focused on the pedagogy of speaking and listening to meet weekly on the campus of Carter Middle School starting in January. The teachers agreed to plan more time for listening and speaking opportunities for their students in the spring as they learned more about how to orchestrate that aspect of the curriculum.

Summary of Evaluation Principles

This example illustrated several important principles that should be kept in mind in all evaluations of school programs. As in other examples in this guide, we provide a list of these principles:

1. Do not attempt to evaluate every aspect of a program at once. Focus the evaluation by selecting a few indicators of quality from the list in Resource A. In this case, the faculty wanted to assess listening and speaking components of the reading and language arts program;

therefore they limited their evaluation to three indicators of those components.

2. When choosing a method of data collection, try to select an alternative that minimizes the burden on those who will be asked to provide information. In this example, a questionnaire allowed all of the teachers to respond when it was convenient for them and did not intrude into their classrooms.

3. Remember that evaluation often requires hard judgments and negative responses that people might be reluctant to express. If at all possible, design the evaluation in ways that permit those who provide information to preserve their privacy. Always guarantee confidentiality. If possible, provide anonymity.

4. Whenever possible, collect information in ways that give every member of the group of interest an opportunity to respond. Remember that you will typically want to draw conclusions about the judgments of "all teachers," "all administrators," or "all students in Grade X." When the group to be represented is small (say, smaller than 100), collecting information from everyone is better than collecting information from a sample. It is difficult to obtain a representative sample when the group to be sampled is small. In this case, the questionnaire was answered by every teacher.

5. Ask questions your information providers are able to answer, and avoid questions that require speculation. Remember that behaviors can be observed, but judgments concerning knowledge are speculative. In this scenario, teachers would have firsthand information about the items as they related to their students.

6. Collect information that will help to identify areas of program success and weakness and guide remedial action when improvement is needed. Certainly, the responses to the questionnaire would identify specific areas in which the teachers perceived weaknesses and thus focus remedial efforts.

7. Whenever possible, seek redundant information. Ask several questions about each important evaluation issue. The questionnaire the evaluation team designed had at least three items per indicator, some negatively stated and some positively stated; therefore the target information was sought several times. Consistent responses to several questions are far more trustworthy than responses to a single question.

Alternatives to the Strategy Used Here

Other Sources and Methods for Collecting Information

Because Indicators 18.2, 18.4, and 18.6 were phrased in terms of evidence of particular components of instruction, teachers were an obvious source of information for assessing these indicators. As discussed earlier, the evaluation team considered the possibilities of collecting judgments from teachers through face-to-face interviews or in a group meeting as well as from classroom observations (perhaps the most appropriate). The evaluation team might have gained additional insights by using any of these data collection strategies after the teachers had completed the anonymous questionnaires. For example, interviews have the advantage of permitting in-depth probing and clarification of initial responses, whereas mailed questionnaires do not. In this evaluation, it would have been useful to obtain information about the types of instructional help the teachers provided students and the experiences from which they felt the students benefited the most. Although the planned professional development opportunities will likely provide a forum for sharing that kind of information, individual interviews might elicit more useful information.

Keep in mind that the objective of this evaluation was to determine if the listening and speaking components of the reading and language arts program provided effective instruction and adequate opportunities for listening and speaking. Identification of strengths and weaknesses in the program enables the school to make improvements where they are needed. Added depth can only help in achieving this objective.

Cautions Regarding Misinterpretation

Limitations of the Questionnaire

It would be easy to summarize the results of this evaluation by concluding that Carter Middle School's listening and speaking program was ineffective. Such a summary is too glib, however, given the data at hand. It is true that most teachers believe the program does not provide instruction to detect propaganda and persuasive language for students. It is also true that most teachers do not believe students receive adequate instruction to give effective oral reports or to organize the information for oral reports. On the other hand, the data were mixed in terms of instruction for students to gather information for oral reports and opportunities for class discussions.

Given that information on each of these issues was collected through three to four questions, the data provided by this evaluation should be regarded as suggestive rather than conclusive. For example, it might not be the case that students lack instruction in organizing information for oral reports. It might be found, upon further investigation, that instruction was delivered in a manner that students were unable to understand. Or it might be found that instruction on organizing information was delivered but students were unable to transfer that instruction to independently prepared reports.

It is also important to remember that this evaluation sought the teachers' perceptions of certain indicators of the listening and speaking components of the reading and language arts program and did not collect data on the students' actual activities or the effectiveness of teachers' instruction. Although teachers' perceptions are critically important, they are not a substitute for information on changes in students' behaviors or abilities that result from the instructional program.

4

Vignette Four

Evaluation of Reading Programs

Where, What, and Why?

Dr. Martin Luther King Middle School was built during the 1960s and currently enrolls about 800 students. When the school was built, most students graduated from high school and attended prestigious universities. Since that time, the neighborhood has experienced many changes, most of which have had detrimental effects on the school. Many families have left for newly developed suburban neighborhoods, leaving behind those who have the least resources. Now, few families own their residences and absentee landlords own most buildings. The neighborhood's quality further deteriorated when city officials allowed an interstate highway to pass through its center. The majority of King's students are black and Hispanic, followed by a small percentage of Asians and caucasians. More than half of the school's families receive some form of government assistance.

Two years ago, community leaders hired Dr. Doris Brown to be the school's principal. She grew up in the neighborhood, had been a successful classroom teacher for 10 years, and recently obtained a doctorate in curriculum and instruction from the local university. When Dr. Brown was hired, faculty morale was extremely low and requests for transfers were higher than at any other school. A teaching position at King Middle School was viewed as one of the least desirable placements in the city. Beginning teachers would take a position at King Middle School only if they couldn't find anything elsewhere.

Community leaders, nevertheless, believed Dr. Brown would serve as a catalyst for changes in their school.

Dr. Brown's positive attitude had an immediate effect. Requests for faculty transfers dropped, the student dropout rate decreased, and parent involvement increased by more than 20%. Dr. Brown was always looking for ways to improve her students' learning and motivation to learn. Over the past year, Dr. Brown and her teachers attended a series of workshops at their local university. These workshops showed teachers how they could use different content area reading strategies during their instruction. Dr. Brown requested the workshops because her teachers believed their students were having difficulty whenever they were asked to complete science and social studies assignments in which a lot of independent reading was required.

A Focus for the Evaluation

To facilitate efforts to improve students' reading comprehension in the content areas, Dr. Brown meets weekly with her teachers to discuss their application of various content area reading strategies. These meetings give teachers an opportunity to design instructional activities and discuss any difficulties they might be experiencing in their classrooms. At a recent meeting, Jean O'Neil, a veteran teacher, mentioned that she had been keeping informal notes on the difficulties students were having with their science and social studies assignments. Over a 3-week period, she had collected her students' assignments to determine which students were experiencing the most difficulties. She concluded that her low- and middle-achieving students were having the most trouble. She believed their problems were related to an inconsistent application of different content reading strategies. She stated, "Some days they can do it, other days they act like they've never seen it before!"

Focusing the Evaluation Ms. O'Neil wondered if there was something else teachers might do to help these students. As she spoke, Dr. Brown was reminded of how teacher expectations had changed at King. She admired how Ms. O'Neil had evaluated her concerns, how she shared this information with colleagues, and her willingness to explore further avenues for improvement. Five years ago, the blame would have been placed on the students. Now teachers were concerned with how they might change their instruction. Who says experienced teachers could not change?

Another teacher agreed with Ms. O'Neil's statements, yet voiced concerns that perhaps expectations were too high. Maybe teachers needed to be more patient, and students would become more successful with time. Others then discussed their reactions to Ms. O'Neil's concerns.

Dr. Brown encouraged this type of discussion because she believed her teachers would be more willing to work toward improving their instruction if they were given opportunities to discuss their views. She listened carefully to her teachers' opinions and encouraged as many individuals as possible as to respond. Each teacher had a vested interest in the school and was encouraged to express his or her views. As Dr. Brown learned in her graduate education, the three keys to effective problem solving were communication, communication, and communication. (See *Evaluating School Programs: An Educator's Guide,* Chapter 2.)

As the meeting neared its end, Dr. Brown already was thinking about how she could use her staff's concerns to improve her science and social studies programs. Dr. Brown summarized the teachers' discussion by stating that there appeared to be a concern that students were not applying different content area reading strategies as effectively as teachers would like and these difficulties were most evident with middle and low achievers. She asked whether her summary was accurate and listened carefully as teachers elaborated on what she had said. Perhaps there was more they could be doing to improve students' reading comprehension in the content areas. Dr. Brown then told teachers they should look more closely at why their students were inconsistently applying their strategies.

Selecting the Evaluation Team

The teachers were receptive to Dr. Brown's suggestion. They knew from previous discussions that her suggestion meant that some of them would be asked to serve on a committee that would meet frequently to study how they should evaluate the program. Ms. O'Neil's informal evaluation of her assignments was a step in the right direction, but it didn't provide the right type of evidence. It was conducted in one classroom with only one teacher. No attempt was made to see if the difficulties Ms. O'Neil perceived existed with all content area reading strategies or only some of them. A more systematic evaluation was needed. Teachers were receptive, in part, because they knew that previous evaluations had led to instructional improvements.

Several considerations have to be made when setting up an evaluation committee. Dr. Brown knew that evaluations depended upon the willingness and expertise of her staff. She had to have someone to chair the committee and direct the evaluation, and she needed to ask people to serve as members of the committee. Committee members needed to have the time to participate in the evaluation and an interest in the evaluation topic. They also needed to have knowledge of how program evaluations were conducted or a willingness to learn. The principal selected Ms. Jean O'Neil as her committee chairperson. Ms. O'Neil was a good person to serve in this role; she had initiated the evaluation by discussing her concerns and was respected by her colleagues. Dr. Brown then asked for two volunteers from each grade level. It was important that each grade have adequate representation so everyone would feel they had input into the evaluation process. (See *Evaluating School Programs: An Educator's Guide,* Chapter 2.)

To begin the evaluation committee's work, Ms. O'Neil knew it was important to get a clear sense of what was to be evaluated. She began the first committee meeting by reviewing those concerns that led to her evaluation effort and asked committee members if they agreed with her observations. Most agreed that they would have come to the same conclusions if they had evaluated their students' class work. In fact, many teachers stated that their students were also able to apply a strategy with one assignment and were at a loss when applying it with another assignment. Ms. O'Neil reviewed the inservice training they received, the goals of which were to provide content area reading strategy instruction so that students could complete assignments successfully and independently. Students initially were expected to apply different strategies under close teacher supervision and then students were expected to apply them more independently over time. This discussion gave committee members a clear understanding of what they needed to evaluate.

The committee still had problems determining why their students were having difficulty consistently applying various content area reading strategies. There were simply far too many reasons that someone might experience difficulties, many of which were not under the school's control. To narrow the evaluation focus, Ms. O'Neil explained that it might be helpful to review a list of standards and indicators of quality reading and language arts programs. Such a list was based on recent research and had been used by previous committees. (See Resource A for this listing.) Ms. O'Neil mentioned that she would send each member a copy of this listing. She asked them to review the list before the next meeting.

Choosing the Standard   As the next meeting began, committee members were discussing which standard they believed to be most relevant to their situation. Their attention was focused particularly on Standard 7, which concerned what students were expected to know as a result of quality instruction. In particular, Indicator 7.2 appeared most appropriate. It stated: "The language arts and reading program shows evidence that students know when and why different reading strategies are used." Perhaps students were experiencing difficulty because they were unaware of when they were supposed to be using different reading strategies or why one strategy was more effective than another. By reviewing these standards and indicators, the committee had narrowed the evaluation's focus and purpose.

Collecting the Information

Even though the evaluation process had just begun, much had been accomplished. A project had been identified, a committee had been selected, and a focus had been determined. The next step was to consider the different ways to collect data to evaluate in terms of Indicator 7.2. Ms. O'Neil listed the different data collection options on a blackboard. She knew that each option needed to be explained in such a manner that the other committee members understood the advantages and disadvantages of each. The committee members did not have to become program evaluation experts, yet they had to have enough knowledge so they could collect information about their program. Their options included collecting work samples (portfolios), distributing a questionnaire, and conducting interviews (individually or in small groups). All of the options appeared to involve considerable effort.

Collecting student work samples was the evaluation committee's first choice because student work was readily available and already collected as part of the school's grading system. This option lost its appeal after committee members realized that student assignments would not give them any clues as to whether or not students understood when and why certain content area reading strategies were to be used. In addition, this measure would probably reinforce what they already knew: Low- and middle-achieving students were having difficulty with science and social studies homework assignments.

Committee members next considered a questionnaire. A questionnaire had the advantage of allowing them to get information from every student in a short period of time. One disadvantage, which eventually turned their interest from this option, was that low- and middle-achieving students might have difficulty writing answers to questionnaire items. Students' responses might not be as elaborate as they would be if students were asked to respond verbally; consequently, the committee would not get information that was rich enough to be useful. Some committee members also believed another disadvantage was that students might say one thing on a questionnaire and perform differently in the actual situation.

Student interviews, an approach that appeared to be the most complex and time consuming, was suddenly becoming the only option. Several options existed if interviews were used. The first option was whether to interview groups or individuals. Group interviews (often referred to as focus groups) quickly were eliminated for many of the reasons that were brought up during the questionnaire discussion. Lower-ability students might not feel comfortable talking in front of their classmates, or they might say one thing during the interview and perform differently when completing assignments. Individual interviews thus were selected as the evaluation method.

The next decision was to determine what they would ask students. They could develop their own questions, or they could see if an interview already existed that could be used. An evaluation committee member came to everyone's rescue when she mentioned that she had read a research article on content area reading strategies as part of an assignment for a graduate course. The article was written by Drs. Gerald Duffy and Laura Roehler, and colleagues, from Michigan State University. They were interested in the same question that the evaluation committee was investigating—whether students understood when and why they were to use a particular reading strategy.

The evaluation committee obtained a copy of the article by Duffy and colleagues (G. Duffy, L. Roehler, M. S. Meloth, R. Polin, G. Rackliffe, A. Tracy, & L. Vavrus, 1987, "Developing and Evaluating Measures Associated with Strategic Reading," *Journal of Reading Behavior, 19,* 223-246). What the researchers found was that students' ability to understand text was related to their understanding of when and why certain reading strategies were used. Students who were able to demonstrate this understanding through interview questions were more likely than classmates to successfully comprehend texts. Evaluation committee members were encouraged by the findings, and they were relieved to see that Duffy and colleagues had streamlined the interview to only three questions. A scoring guide also was provided to evaluate students' interview responses.

Questions remained about how the evaluation committee might use the questionnaire. For example, they needed to decide if they would interview students about one or several content reading strategies. If the evaluation committee concentrated on one strategy, their task would be easier than if they examined many different strategies because students would only be interviewed about one assignment. This approach would take far less time than would several interviews. The disadvantage, of course, was that what might be true for one strategy might not be true for another. The evaluation committee decided that they should interview students about three strategies. It would take a longer period of time to conduct the interviews, yet teachers would have a more accurate picture of any difficulties their students were experiencing.

The evaluation committee then focused on the question of how many students they would interview. There were 24 classrooms with 25 to 30 students in each. It was decided that they would interview 9 students from each classroom (3 each of low, average, and high achievers). Students were placed into one of the three achievement levels based on standardized test scores, and names were selected randomly from each list. This procedure guaranteed that every student would have an equal chance of being selected.

Creating the Interview   The evaluation committee experimented with the interview and found that each interview could be conducted in 3 minutes. Evaluation committee members estimated that three students could be interviewed each day so that all interviews for each class should be completed within a 2-week period. They wanted to hire a consultant from outside the school to conduct the interviews but were unable to do this because King Middle School lacked the financial resources for a consultant. As a result, the evaluation committee decided that teachers would interview students from classrooms other than their own. Committee members described their plan to other teachers in their grade levels and asked whether they believed it could be carried out. The other teachers were willing to interview students and approved their plan.

When coding the interview, Ms. O'Neil told committee members that students' names should be crossed out and identification numbers used. Committee members would then code responses according to the criteria developed by Duffy and colleagues. To limit the possibility that coding would be influenced by opinion or by an inappropriate application of the coding criteria, it was recommended that interviews should be coded twice at the start of the coding and at scheduled intervals thereafter. For similar reasons, Ms. O'Neil suggested that teachers should not code the student interviews from their own grades.

Students would be asked three questions from the Duffy et al. questionnaire that were modified by the evaluation committee. The first question was this: "What strategy did you use when completing this assignment?" The second question: "When are you supposed to use this strategy?" The third question: "Why is this strategy a good one to use with this assignment?"

The first question measured whether students were aware of the strategy that was required to complete the assignment. If the students identified the correct strategy after Question 1, then they would be asked Questions 2 (when) and 3 (why), which would then be evaluated according to the following 5-point scale. Possible student responses for each level are in the parentheses.

Level 1 (L1): No awareness or includes no reference to the specific task. ("It'll help me when I grow up.")

Level 2 (L2): The response is not specific to the task but is related to reading-language arts generally. ("I'll read better.")

Level 3 (L3): The response refers to an appropriate general category but not to the specific use for what was taught. ("I can read science books better.")

Level 4 (L4): The response includes specific reference to what he or she will be able to do but not the context in which it would be useful. ("When I come to a science paragraph I can use this strategy.")

Level 5 (L5): The response includes both what he or she will be able to do and the context within which it is useful. ("When I read a difficult science paragraph, this strategy will help me to predict what will come next and identify any parts I need to reread.")

TABLE 4.1   Percentage of Students by Achievement Level for Assignment 1

Achievement Level	Knowledge of When a Strategy Is Used					Knowledge of Why a Strategy Is Used				
Level of Understanding	1	2	3	4	5	1	2	3	4	5
Low achievers	30	30	20	15	5	25	35	15	20	5
Average achievers	5	10	20	45	20	5	15	25	40	15
High achievers	0	0	5	15	80	5	5	0	5	85

Organizing and Analyzing Information

The interviews were completed during a 2-week period. Following Ms. O'Neil's recommendations, teachers from different grades exchanged students' responses so that they did not evaluate their own students' interviews. The next step was to evaluate interview responses using Duffy and colleagues' criteria (Level 1—no awareness—through Level 5—sophisticated understanding of strategy use). Interviews were divided into five stacks, one for each of the scoring levels. Each interview was coded by two different people to make sure teachers placed interviews consistently into one of the five response levels. Immediately after completing this step, teachers realized that there were unequal numbers of interviews at each level, an indication that students had different levels of understanding about when and why a particular strategy was used. Committee members then looked at whether there were differences by achievement level. To complete this step, they referred back to the identification numbers to discover each student's achievement level and counted the number of students at each level. The results of this analysis for the first reading strategy are presented in Table 4.1 according to the percentage of responses that fell into each of the five response levels.

Interpreting the Data   These results indicated that there were differences among students' understanding of when and why a particular strategy was used, and these differences were related to students' general achievement levels. For example, the majority of low achievers (60%) tended to be placed in response Levels 1 and 2 on both questions. Fewer medium-achieving students were placed at this level as the majority of their responses (65%) were at response Levels 3 and 4. High-achieving students generally were placed in response Level 5 (85%). This trend indicated that low and middle achievers were far less likely than high achievers to have an understanding of when and why content strategy 1 was used.

Reporting Information

The results confirmed teachers' perceptions that students were having difficulty completing homework assignments because of their understanding of different reading strategies. They also gave committee members a possible explanation for why students were having difficulty. One needs to be careful here not to assume that, if an evaluation finds something missing, teachers simply need to direct their attentions toward this area. The reason for this caution is that many factors affect actual performance, some of which teachers cannot control. Some other factor that wasn't measured might also help to explain why students experienced difficulty. It would be naive to assume a simple cause-effect relation between performance and student understanding (e.g., reading comprehension performance and understanding of when and why a strategy would be used).

Sharing the Information

The final step was to prepare a report. As soon as the report was completed, they would share it with individuals who were not on the committee. The reason for sharing a draft report was that someone might have a different interpretation of the results and should be allowed to voice them. In addition, even the committee members might reach different conclusions after they had a chance to think about their work. At a final meeting, Dr. Brown thanked Ms. Jean O'Neil and her teachers for serving on the committee. Dr. Brown then suggested that their next step would be to increase their students' understanding of when and why content area reading strategies were used. Ms. O'Neil suggested that teachers could receive inservice that specifically focused on how they could increase student understanding of when and why certain reading strategies were used. The second option would be to read more research on the topic or to ask the researchers whose interviews they used to speak to the teachers.

Summary of Evaluation Principles

This example illustrated several important principles that should be kept in mind in all evaluations of school programs. As in other examples in this guide, we provide a list of these principles.

1. Do not attempt to evaluate every aspect of the program at once. Focus the evaluation by selecting a few indicators of quality from the list in

Resource A or from other resources. In this vignette, the teachers were able to narrow their focus by examining standards and indicators of a quality language arts program.

2. When choosing a method of data collection, try to select an alternative that minimizes the burden on those who will provide information and can be implemented given your resources and timetable. In this vignette, interviews were used. Committee members made their task easier by finding an interview that had been tested by noted researchers.

3. Remember that evaluation often requires hard judgments and negative responses that people might be reluctant to express. If at all possible, design the evaluation in ways that permit those who provide information to preserve their privacy. Always guarantee confidentiality. If possible, provide anonymity. The evaluation committee attended to this point by giving students identification numbers and crossing out their names. They also provided anonymity by presenting data for the school and not by individual classes.

4. Ask questions your information providers are able to answer, and avoid questions that require speculation. Remember that behaviors can be observed, but judgments concerning knowledge are speculative. The evaluation committee avoided these problems by using interview questions that had been tested by others.

5. When conducting interviews, make sure everyone practices the procedure before the evaluation begins. When evaluating your data, make sure everyone is applying the scoring criteria the same way (double code some of the data). You should have at least 90% accuracy; in most cases, disagreements should be resolved through discussion. The committee followed this principle by pilot testing the interview and by using two coders when evaluating students' responses.

Alternatives to the Strategy Used Here

The optimal strategy for this evaluation was to interview the students. This was the best measure because the indicator required evidence that students understood when and why they used a particular reading strategy. No other measure would provide this type of information. If teachers used the evaluation results to alter their instruction so that students would develop a clearer understanding of when and why a strategy was used, then it might be feasible to follow up with other measures. For example, after attempting to increase their students' understanding of when and why a strategy was used, the evaluation committee might then want to collect assignments to see if their students' ability to apply reading strategies in the content area improved accordingly. The point is that students might develop an understanding of when and why a strategy is used and still not be able to apply it successfully in a variety of situations. Other factors such as student developmental level and the assignment's difficulty level affect knowledge maintenance and transfer.

Cautions Regarding Misinterpretation

The most common misinterpretation of these findings would be if committee members assumed that student reading performances, especially those measured by standardized performance tests, would improve if students' understanding of when and why a particular strategy is used improves. Reading performances are affected by many factors and teachers do not have control over all of them. Furthermore, while student understanding is important, it is not a substitute for actual changes in their performance.

5

Vignette Five

Evaluation of Writing Programs

Where, What, and Why?

Built in the mid-1970s, the Barbara Jordan Senior High School is centrally located in a large metropolitan area in south Texas with a population of about 250,000. The school enrolls 974 students in Grades 9 through 12, some of whom are bused to Jordan High School from white-collar suburban areas. Although the school's immediate environment is primarily populated by blue-collar workers, most of whom own their homes, Jordan High School also draws students from a subsidized housing area for low-income renters. Given the three distinct student populations, the school is racially as well as socioeconomically diverse. About 30% of the students are black, 15% are Hispanic, 3% are Asian, and 52% are white.

In his 6 years as the principal of Jordan High School, David Summers has established a positive educational climate with his staff of 48 classroom teachers, 2 media specialists, 2 reading specialists, 3 special education teachers, a vice principal, and 3 school counselors for the students. The staff is committed to high quality education, parental involvement, and students' interpersonal growth and development. In fact, Mr. Summers prides himself on Jordan High School's low dropout rate and high college entrance rate, given the makeup of the student population. Mr. Summers credits those records to the staff's willingness to work to improve the effectiveness of the school instructional programs through a continuing program of selective, systematic, and focussed evaluations. Because the teachers see Mr. Summers as fair, supportive, and interested in the students, they are willing to participate in ongoing program evaluation in all of the curricular areas. At Jordan High School, program evaluation has been a way to identify poor educational practices that can then be changed or modified. As a result, curricular decisions are informed by systematically collected data, although program evaluations also may be used for other purposes (see *Evaluating School Programs: An Educator's Guide,* Chapter 2).

The previous year, the district committed to a Writing Across the Curriculum program. The purposes of a Writing Across the Curriculum program are to help students master the content of the curriculum, improve their writing skills, increase thinking skills, as well as experience a variety of contexts for writing. The district's leaders also hoped that teachers would come to see writing as a way to prepare students for success in the workplace or college. For example, when students write in the various subject areas, teachers would create writing assignments that parallel "real life" writing: A science teacher might ask students to pretend to be a laboratory technician preparing a report for his or her company's marketing department explaining the results of the experimental testing of a new product.

A Focus for the Evaluation

Focusing the Evaluation   Prior to the first August back-to-school faculty meeting, Mr. Summers alerted the faculty that the agenda for the meeting included a discussion of the ongoing program evaluation of the school's curricula. Given that the faculty, as stakeholders who have a strong interest in the quality of the school's programs, would have differing views about what the next evaluation focus should be, he was concerned that they have plenty of time to think about their needs and preferences. The teachers knew from the previous year that a program evaluation was not aimed at evaluating them but the target program itself. At the meeting, the teachers suggested the general focus of evaluation this year should be the school's Writing Across the Curriculum program that was implemented last year. Their suggestion reflected their belief that writing competence was important for their students and that an evaluation of the writing program would help them locate any difficulties—with their students ultimately benefiting from the effort.

As the faculty discussed the school's efforts to improve students' writing skills across the various curricular areas, they were able to focus their concerns. For instance, during the initial phase of the discussion, they clearly were not particularly pleased with their efforts the first year of the program but did not know what aspect of the Writing Across the Curriculum program needed to be improved. As the discussion continued, some of the subject area teachers admitted that, although they had time to have their students write, they rarely did because they felt that their assignments were just "more of the same." That is, they just told their students to write about whatever topic they were studying. Although the English teachers claimed to have had students complete writing assignments on a regular basis, even they were not always comfortable with the quality of their assignments. After much sharing and clarifying, the faculty determined that their primary concern was about the quality of the writing assignments they gave the students.

Selecting an Evaluation Team

Mr. Summers asked Ms. Ault, the vice principal and curriculum leader, to be in charge of the evaluation committee because of her expertise and training in evaluation and curriculum. Ms. Ault knew that committee members should be interested, have the time, and also be knowledgeable about writing and, she hoped, program evaluation procedures. She also knew that teachers could learn enough about evaluation to do the job by studying this guide and *Evaluating School Programs: An Educator's Guide* in this series. Ms. Ault asked the heads of the English, science, and social studies departments for names of teachers in their departments who might be knowledgeable and interested in being on the evaluation team. Mr. Tucker, an English teacher, and Ms. Chang, a science teacher, volunteered. Ms. Forester and Ms. Davidson, the two reading-language arts specialists, also volunteered. The social studies teachers were involved with textbook adoption for the coming year so were willing to leave the evaluation effort to the four selected teachers. Nevertheless, all of the teachers as stakeholders recognized the value of an effective writing program and thus the need to devote extra time to an evaluation effort that would ultimately help their students.

Selecting the Indicator to Evaluate

A writing program is complex. It includes notions about the time spent writing, the instruction provided students, the characteristics of the writing process, the information that should be included in writing assignments, the forms discourse takes, and the conventions of writing (i.e., spelling, punctuation, language usage, and penmanship). To gain a clear sense of what was to be evaluated, at the first evaluation committee meeting, Ms. Ault suggested that they begin by reviewing the writing literature and then consider the standards and indicators of quality reading and language arts programs provided in Resource A of this guide and based on writing research. Ms. Ault believed that the team needed a foundation upon which to base their decision about what specifically to evaluate in the writing assignments. They also needed to relate the information to the resources and personnel available (see *Evaluating School Programs: An Educator's Guide,* Chapter 2).

After reading a review of the writing literature, they understood that effective writing assignments clearly indicate the voice that the writer needs to strive for (i.e., the persona or the personality a writer projects through his or her writing) and the topic that the writer should address. They also learned that writing assignments should indicate the audience for whom the writer is writing, which has an effect on both the form and the content of the text. Finally, writing assignments should indicate the purpose of the text, thereby shaping the text. The purpose of the assignment determines whether the text is an expressive, informative, or persuasive piece. The mode of the text, or method of organization, is linked closely to the purpose (e.g., texts might be organized as narrations, descriptions, classifications, or evaluations). For instance, the science teacher who asks students to pretend to be a laboratory technician (voice) preparing a report (text) for his or her company's marketing department (audience) explaining the results of experimental testing of a new product (topic) so that new production decisions can be made (purpose) would have provided a writing assignment with the needed components.

Ms. Ault and the teachers then discussed the list of standards and indicators of a quality writing program (see Resource A) to help clarify their focus as well as reduce any interpretive differences among the committee members. She wanted each member of the evaluation committee to understand the language in the indicators in the same way. Finally, they selected Indicator 15.1—"The language arts and reading program provides evidence that writing assignments are focused to include information about the required voice, topic, audience, and text." Because writing assignments that varied on these factors seemed so important to an effective Writing Across the Curriculum program, the team thought Indicator 15.1 was an important point at which to begin their evaluation. Deficiencies on this indicator would argue that the needed variety of writing opportunities that the teachers believed students should experience would be lacking.

Collecting Information

Choosing a Data Collection Instrument

Certainly, evaluating the writing program at Jordan High School would take time and money, both of which were in short supply. The evaluation team therefore carefully considered what information they needed to assess Indicator 15.1 and ways to gather that information (see *Evaluating School Programs: An Educator's Guide,* Chapter 3). It was clear from the wording of the indicator that they had to consider the writing assignments that the teachers gave the students. There are different ways to collect information, each of which has its advantages and disadvantages. For example, they thought about interviewing a few teachers from each department during their free period but rejected the idea because they knew that "a few" teachers might not reflect the practice of all the teachers at Jordan High School, thus limiting the reliability of the evaluation. They also rejected using interviews because of other problems that would affect the validity of the evaluation: Teachers would be reluctant to give up their free periods and also might not be completely frank during the interview because it would not be anonymous (we all present ourselves in the best possible way). The evaluation team also considered a student questionnaire that asked students about their writing assignments. The notion of a questionnaire was rejected because the evaluation team did not believe students were knowledgeable enough about the desired elements in a writing assignment to respond accurately. The team then considered classroom observations but quickly rejected that option because of the cost in money and time.

After rejecting these alternatives, Ms. Forester remembered reading about using portfolios as an evaluation tool. She explained that a portfolio was a collection of a person's work. For example, if teachers prepared portfolios about their teaching skills, they might include a video of their teaching a lesson, their lesson plans, student evaluations, thoughts on what was happening in their classrooms, or other evidence of their teaching. The team then read what they could find on portfolios in professional journals. From their reading, they learned that the portfolios might also include artifacts of planning and teaching, such as an overview of 3 to 5 weeks of instruction, resources, a teaching unit, student handouts, and/or samples of student assignments and student work. Portfolios might contain reflections about why teachers made the instructional decisions they made. They could include planning journals or logs that recorded reasons for instructional adjustments in lesson plans, for information learned, or for persisting problems.

Designing the Portfolio   Ms. Forester suggested they ask teachers to create special portfolios that focused on the writing assignments in their classrooms. The team concurred but believed that they should collect six assignments per teacher to have enough data to fairly represent the assignments students were receiving. Consequently, the team agreed to ask the teachers to include in the portfolios all of their writing assignments over a 3-month period. They reasoned that, if teachers usually gave a writing assignment every 2 weeks, a 3-month period would probably produce about six assignments per teacher (even though they suspected that most teachers gave far fewer assignments than that).

This approach had several advantages compared with the rejected alternatives. The portfolios would enable the team to consider the actual writing assignments used in each classroom and determine if they included information about voice, topic, audience, and text. That is, when they considered the data in the portfolios, the evaluation team would be able to focus on specific elements in the writing assignments that would measure Indicator 15.1 in a way that would ensure the validity of the evaluation.

The next question the evaluation team discussed was whether to evaluate all the writing assignments for the 3-month period or just a representative sample of them (see *Evaluating School Programs: An Educator's Guide,* Chapter 3). The evaluation team thought a sample would be sufficient to draw conclusions about the writing assignments if there were representative samples of all the subject areas. Thus they planned to sample portfolios randomly from each subject area rather than consider data from all of them. When the committee consulted several program evaluation books, however, they found the authors recommended collecting information from everyone if the group being sampled was smaller than 100 (see *Evaluating School Programs: An Educator's Guide,* Chapter 2). It is difficult to obtain a representative sample when the group being sampled is small. As a result of this recommendation, Ms. Ault suggested that it would be time consuming but far wiser to collect data from every teacher, ensuring the reliability of the evaluation.

Mr. Summers asked Ms. Ault to explain at the next faculty meeting what the evaluation team recommended and secure the cooperation of all the teachers to prepare portfolios that reflected the writing programs in their classrooms. He knew a number of things could go wrong when collecting data and cautioned the committee to try to anticipate any problems (see *Evaluating School Programs: An Educator's Guide,* Chapter 3). The evaluation team agreed to provide a short presentation at the next faculty meeting about portfolios so that the teachers would feel confident as they created theirs.

The evaluation team prepared the faculty presentation about portfolios. In their presentation to the faculty, the evaluation team members asked that the portfolios cover the next 3 months and urged the teachers to include all of their writing assignments in the portfolios because the assignments would be the focus of the evaluation team.

Organizing and Analyzing Information

Organizing the Data   While the teachers were compiling their portfolios, the members of the evaluation team created a form to help them when they analyzed the teachers' writing assignments. Because they had decided to evaluate all the writing assignments, they needed a quick way to organize the data (see *Evaluating School Programs: An Educator's Guide,* Chapter 4), as shown in Table 5.1.

By the end of the 3 months, the teachers had compiled portfolios that contained the writing assignments given in their classrooms; therefore the evaluation team could begin their data compilation. The

TABLE 5.1   Writing Assignment Analysis Form

Grade _____ Subject Area _____ Teacher Number _____

Assignment/Date	Voice	Topic	Audience	Purpose	Text
Assignment 1					
Assignment 2					
Assignment 3					
Assignment 4					
Assignment 5					
Assignment 6					

evaluation team first reviewed the definitions of the recommended criteria for writing assignments. They remembered that a writing assignment had to indicate clearly the voice that the writer needed to strive for (i.e., the persona or the personality a writer projects through his or her writing) and the topic the writer should address. The writing assignment also needed to indicate the audience for which the writer was writing, which has an effect on both the form and the content of a text. Finally, the writing assignments had to indicate the purpose of the text, which determines whether the text is an expressive, informative, or persuasive piece. The purpose of the text also defines its organization, such as a narrative text, a descriptive text, a classificatory text, or an evaluative text.

The evaluation team realized that they needed to be consistent as they judged the writing assignments. In other words, each team member had to apply the same criteria as the other team member applied to the writing assignments. Ms. Davidson and Ms. Forester assigned a number to each teacher and his or her portfolio. Each team member then evaluated the same three writing assignments and compared their findings, resolving any disagreements. For the remaining writing assignment, they agreed that each assignment would be evaluated by two team members to check for consistency. If a disagreement occurred, a third team member would evaluate the assignment.

Interpreting the Data

Finally, the team began evaluating the writing assignments. After all the writing assignments had been evaluated, the evaluation team discussed the data. They realized that, if they computed the percentage of critical elements present in the writing assignments they evaluated, they would have a clearer picture of the assignments students received during the past 3 months than if they simply presented tallies. Ms. Davidson volunteered to compute the percentages for the total number (schoolwide) of writing assignments as well as the percentages for each content area. She believed, if the figures were available by content areas as well, Mr. Summers and Ms. Ault could use the

TABLE 5.2   Results of Writing Assignment Analysis

Subject Area	Number of Teachers	Assignment	Voice		Topic		Audience		Text		Purpose
English	8	48	30	(63%)	37	(77%)	31 (65%)	48 (100%)		37 (77%)
Social Studies	10	30	2	(7%)	30 (100%)		2	(7%)	30 (100%)		15 (50%)
Science	6	6	0		6 (100%)		0		4	(67%)	2 (33%)
Health/PE	6	6	0		6 (100%)		5 (83%)		5	(83%)	2 (33%)
Speech/ Drama	2	4	3	(75%)	1	(25%)	3 (75%)	3 (75%)		1 (25%)
Art	1	2	0		2 (100%)		0		0		1 (50%)
Technology	3	3	0		3 (100%)		0		2	(67%)	2 (67%)
Math	8	8	0		8 (100%)		0		0		0
Music	2	4	0		2	(50%)	0		1	(25%)	0
Business	1	3	0		0		2 (67%)	3 (100%)		2 (67%)
Foreign Language	1	2	2 (100%)		2 (100%)		0		0		0
Totals	48	116	37	(32%)	97	(84%)	43 (37%)	96	(83%)		62 (54%)

results to provide support and guidance where it was most needed (see *Evaluating School Programs: An Educator's Guide*, Chapter 4). Ms. Davidson's computations are shown in Table 5.2.

In the format Ms. Davidson chose, the results seemed to be easy for the faculty to understand. As the evaluation team studied the results, Ms. Forester wondered what the average number of writing assignments was schoolwide. After further calculations, the evaluation team determined that, in 3 months, the 48 faculty members gave students an average of 2.4 writing assignments.

Reporting Information

Sharing the Information

The stakeholders should be kept informed about the evaluation process and progress being made toward its completion. In this case, the teachers' portfolios, designed to assess Indicator 15.1, contained the writing assignments they gave their students during a 3-month period. Recall that the indicator stated "writing assignments . . . include information about the required voice, topic, audience, and text." The table was chosen to report the data because it reflected how many teachers Jordan High School employed, by subject area, the number of writing assignments given in each subject area, and the percentage of times the assignments indicated the voice, topic, audience, text, and/ or purpose that students were to address in their compositions.

When the team considered the characteristics of the writing assignments across subject areas, it was obvious that the teachers as a group were not indicating the voice or the audience in their assignments of which students should be cognizant as they composed. For instance, only 32% of the writing assignments indicated the voice, and only 37% of the assignments included the audience for which the students were writing. On the other hand, the teachers were usually providing students with the topic about which they were to write (84% of the time). This was not surprising because, with a Writing Across the Curriculum program, the teachers would have their students acquire a deeper understanding of particular topics in their subject area by writing about them. The data suggested by the teachers provided students with the purpose of the assignment 62% of the time and did fairly well indicating the mode (or organization) of text students were to compose (83%). These latter results was also not surprising because the evaluation team knew that subject area teachers who gave writing assignments would probably indicate whether students were to write a report, a persuasive piece, a critique, a summary, a letter, a story, a poem, and so on.

When the results were considered by subject area, the team concluded that there were subject areas that seemed to have a greater need for improvement than other areas. For example, the science, health/PE, technology, and math teachers gave few writing assignments; moreover, those subject area teachers as well as the art and music teachers never indicated the voice or the audience in their assignments.

Making Decisions Based on the Information

With the notion of improving the teachers' ability to provide writing assignments that included information about voice, topic, audience, text, and purpose, Mr. Summer arranged a full faculty meeting so that the evaluation team could share their findings with their colleagues. Another purpose of the meeting was to develop an improvement strategy. Ms. Ault conducted the meeting and began by discussing positive findings. For instance, the teachers as a whole included information about the topics on which they wanted their students to write as well as the kind of text they wanted to see as the finished composition. Ms. Ault also discussed briefly why it was important to include these elements in assignments for students. She then shared the evaluation results about the inclusion of information about the voice writers would use and the audience for which writers would write. The results validated the faculty's initial concerns, indicating a clear need to increase the teachers' competence in creating writing assignments. The need, moreover, was greater in some subject areas than others.

As a result of the meeting, the English teachers volunteered to help other teachers develop writing assignments that included the necessary elements. The art, music, and speech/drama teachers agreed to form an arts study group to take advantage of their colleagues' offer.

Furthermore, Mr. Summer agreed to obtain funds from the central administration to support a staff development program that focused on Writing Across the Curriculum. He particularly wanted the program to include information on framing writing assignments that were appropriate for the subject areas and that included information about voice, topic, audience, text, and purpose for the writer. The teachers were interested in the staff development program because it promised to be relevant to their subject areas and needs. They were also pleased that constructive responses to the results of the evaluation were developed.

Summary of Evaluation Principles

This example illustrated several important principles that should be kept in mind in all evaluations of school programs (see *Evaluating School Programs: An Educator's Guide*). As in other examples in this guide, we provide a list of these principles:

1. Do not attempt to evaluate every aspect of a program at once. Focus the evaluation by selecting a few indicators of quality from the list in Resource A. For example, the teachers at Barbara Jordan Senior High School wanted to consider the components of their writing assignments; therefore they selected an indicator that reflected their concern.

2. When choosing a method of data collection, try to select an alternative that minimizes the burden on those who will be asked to provide information but provides the needed information. In this case, the teachers simply have to drop a copy of their assignments into their portfolios.

3. Remember that evaluation often requires hard judgments and negative responses that people might be reluctant to express. If at all possible, design the evaluation in ways that permit those who provide information to preserve their privacy. Always try to guarantee confidentiality. If possible, provide anonymity. In this scenario, it was not possible to provide anonymity because several subject areas had only one teacher; however, confidentiality was guaranteed.

4. Whenever possible, collect information in ways that give every member of the group of interest an opportunity to respond. Remember that you typically will want to draw conclusions about the judgments of "all teachers," "all administrators," or "all students in Grade X." When the group to be represented is small (say, fewer than 100), collecting information from everyone is better than collecting information from a sample. It is difficult to obtain a representative sample when the group to be sampled is small. In this case, the evaluation team collected portfolios from all of the teachers.

5. Ask for information providers are able to provide and avoid requests that require speculation. Remember that behaviors can be observed,

but judgments concerning knowledge are speculative. For this indicator, use of portfolios with teachers' writing assignments was a straightforward way to gather information.

6. Collect information that will help to identify areas of program success and weakness and guide remedial action when improvement is needed. Because the portfolios could be sorted by subject, curricular areas in need of improvement could easily be identified.

7. Whenever possible, seek redundant information. Ask for information about each evaluation issue and seek information from more than one source. Consistent information from several sources is more trustworthy than information from a single source. Consistent responses to several questions are far more trustworthy than responses to a single question. Certainly, the portfolios from across the curriculum provided the evaluation team with both redundant information (they had several assignments from each source) and information from more than one source (all curricular areas were evaluated).

8. When evaluating information across portfolios, organize the information around the question you are seeking to answer. In this case, the writing assignments were collected and components of the assignments were evaluated. The data were organized by components of the writing assignments across subject areas as well as by subject areas.

Alternatives to the Strategy Used Here

Other Sources and Methods of Collecting Information

Because Indicator 15.1 was phrased in terms of evidence of components of writing assignments, the actual writing assignments were the obvious source of information for assessing this indicator. As discussed earlier, the evaluation team considered and rejected the possibilities of collecting information about the critical components from teachers through face-to-face interviews, observations, or questionnaires. The evaluation team might have gained additional insights, however, by using interviews after the teachers had completed their portfolios containing their writing assignments. Interviews have the advantage of permitting in-depth probing and clarification of initial information, whereas portfolios or observations do not. In this evaluation, it was useful to obtain information on the way each subject area was implementing the Writing Across the Curriculum program. Keep in mind that the objective of this evaluation was identification of the components of writing assignments so that the writing program could be improved.

Cautions Regarding Misinterpretation

It would be easy to summarize the results of this evaluation by concluding that Barbara Jordan High School was not providing writing assignments containing the necessary components; moreover, certain subject area teachers were responsible for most of the difficulties exposed by the evaluation. Such a summary, however, is certainly too glib given the data. It is true that the English teachers seemed to be providing more complete writing assignments in terms of the voice, topic, audience, text, and purpose, but information was collected with one instrument during one 3-month period. It might not be the case if the data had been collected 2 months earlier or later.

Limitations of the Portfolios

It is also important to remember that this evaluation did not touch on whether students understand these components of a composition or on how students are instructed to address these components when they are included in an assignment. It also did not consider if or how well students' compositions reflect these components. This evaluation only considered the writing assignments teachers' gave during a 3-month period. The next step for the evaluation team might be to determine how much time is allocated to writing instruction and to consider the instruction that occurs during the time scheduled for writing instruction.

6

Vignette Six

Evaluation of an Integrated Reading and Language Arts Program

Where, What, and Why?

Kent County School District is 40 miles west of a large metropolitan area. Two industries, a brewery and a fabric mill, support the local economy. Most families work in one of these industries or own a local business that provides related services. Except for upper-level management families, most people have lived in the area for several generations. There are four elementary schools, two middle schools, and a high school. Students come from blue-collar families, and the majority of them are white.

The pressures on Kent County educational administrators to improve the quality of their instruction have increased consistently over the past 10 years. These pressures are related to a concern that students need a better education to participate in the local economies. No longer can an individual quit school or obtain a high school diploma and enter local industries with the belief that he or she will be employed for life. To enter these industries, one must understand how to operate sophisticated machines and other technologies, abilities that require high-level literacy skills. Furthermore, due to the implementation of site-based management, workers now must know how to work together while demonstrating these skills. To be assured of long-term employment, workers must be able to develop abilities that were not required in previous years.

A Focus for the Evaluation

The pressures on the educators to improve the quality of their instruction has led to much discussion and the examination of several educational alternatives. Teachers have been encouraged to have their students write and read more frequently and study together for extended period of times. At the monthly meeting of school administrators, three elementary school principals stated that several of their fourth- and fifth-grade teachers had returned from an inservice workshop on an integrated reading and language arts curriculum and reported that this instructional alternative would enable the Kent County schools to better meet the educational needs of their students.

The superintendent, Dr. Lucretia Noyse, asked her coordinator for reading and language arts, Dr. Alice Goodier, to comment on the types of changes that might occur with an integrated curriculum. Dr. Noyse realized there was interest at the state level to move in this direction and wanted to better understand the differences between an integrated reading and language arts curriculum and their current reading and language arts curriculum. Without this understanding, it would be difficult for her to support an effort to move toward an integrated curriculum, to explain to concerned parents the benefits of such a change, or to estimate the types of resources she would have to allocate to support a change.

Focusing the Evaluation Dr. Goodier stated that an integrated curriculum had been gaining acceptance in recent years. She further stated that this approach was similar in many ways to literature-based or whole-language instruction. She explained that an integrated reading and language arts curriculum was primarily found in the primary grades (K-2) and that differences between a standard and an integrated curriculum were related to how different skills were presented and practiced. With the standard curriculum, skills were presented in isolation, which meant that a number of different skills typically were presented each day. As a result, students often completed several assignments each day. Also, subject areas (reading, language arts, social studies, science, and so on) were presented as separate disciplines; little, if any, effort was made to show how the skills learned in one area might apply to another. On the other hand, with an integrated curriculum, assignments usually focused on more than one skill and often involved more than one curricular area. Furthermore, because skills were not practiced in isolation, there was a greater emphasis placed on the demonstration of sophisticated writing skills. As a result, students often worked on the same assignment for several days. The integrated curriculum was thought to increase student understanding of how they could apply what they were learning to a variety of situations in different curricular areas. Dr. Goodier finished her explanation by mentioning how state officials were indeed interested in determining how many of its teachers were moving in this direction. She added her belief that this approach did give students more opportunities to write and read extended prose and study collaboratively.

Some elementary principals responded to Dr. Goodier's comments by stating that some of their teachers were using a standard approach while others were integrating their instruction (sometimes including science and social studies). Dr. Goodier agreed that there were differences among teachers' existing practices and that many teachers probably were using some form of an integrated curriculum. She then recommended that a committee should be established to evaluate the current uses of an integrated reading and language arts curriculum in their schools. This information would help her to address the state's concerns and would help the superintendent and principals assist teachers who might want to move in this direction.

Evaluating a reading and language arts program is a complex task, one that could require the efforts of many teachers and administrators as well as resources that might be used for other purposes. The first step for the Kent County schools was to form an evaluation committee that would develop goals and a timetable for reaching them (see *Evaluating School Programs: An Educator's Guide,* Chapter 2). The principals, coordinator, and superintendent agreed that it would probably be best to ask for volunteers from those schools where there was interest in an integrated curriculum because interested teachers probably would have more motivation to serve on such a committee. In addition to interested teachers, the principals also were asked to solicit assistance from teachers who had experience with previous program evaluations.

Selecting the Evaluation Team

Dr. Noyse suggested that Dr. Goodier serve as the evaluation committee chairperson and that members should be selected from interested schools. Each principal mentioned the committee's purpose at his or her next faculty meeting and asked for teachers who were interested in an integrated reading and language arts curriculum to volunteer. The principals further stated that the meetings would be after school on Tuesdays and that the committee had to finish its evaluation before the end of the school year. They mentioned these facts so that the teachers knew what was expected and could decide if they had the time available to participate. It is often easier to express a desire to do something than it is to find the time to participate. Fourteen teachers from the four schools as well as two assistant principals volunteered to serve on the evaluation committee.

The evaluation committee had to answer many questions so that they could make decisions that were informed and supportable. For example, how does one define an integrated curriculum? Does this definition change according to a student's grade level? What are the different ways in which an integrated curriculum could be evaluated? How long would an evaluation take? What constraints must one consider when developing an evaluation plan? How would the results of such an effort be used? The committee had to develop a clear understanding of how they would attempt to answer each of these questions; otherwise, each member might have a different understanding of the committee's purpose. (See *Evaluating School Programs: An Educator's Guide,* Chapter 2.)

At the first meeting, Dr. Alice Goodier described the events that had led to the establishment of an evaluation committee. She further explained that the committee's task was to obtain information about the extent to which teachers in the district already were using an integrated reading and language arts curriculum. The evaluation committee's charge was not to endorse or promote one type of instruction over another. They simply were to obtain information that later could be used to determine the appropriateness of one instructional approach over another. She then asked teachers to write down their definition of an integrated reading and language arts curriculum and to explain how this definition differed from a standard reading and language arts curriculum. Each teacher discussed his or her definitions and it soon became obvious why Dr. Goodier had conducted this activity. The evaluation committee members did not share common definitions of what integrated and traditional curricula were. Without this common understanding, it would be difficult to proceed because everyone would be thinking of different things while evaluating the same curriculum.

Another reason for conducting this discussion was Dr. Goodier's belief that evaluation committee members would be more willing to participate if they were allowed to voice their opinions and share responsibilities. Because everyone on the committee had a strong interest in what they were evaluating and knew that their opinions would be considered, they welcomed the opportunity to participate in the discussion. (See *Evaluating School Programs: An Educator's Guide,* Chapter 2.)

To help further identify the components of an integrated curriculum, Dr. Goodier shared research articles on this topic with the evaluation committee. The articles helped committee members define differences between integrated and standard reading and language arts curricula and the ways in which an integrated curriculum was implemented. The committee members were asked to read them and write down how their definitions of an integrated reading and language arts curriculum changed as a result of this new information. After reviewing the articles, three criteria were identified as critical to any definition of an integrated curriculum. An integrated curriculum included more than one skill within a particular assignment, emphasized the relationship among different disciplines (e.g., science, social studies), and offered students extended opportunities to develop their speaking and listening abilities.

Deciding on an Indicator

Dr. Goodier then asked the evaluation committee to review the standards and indicators of successful reading and language arts programs in Resource A of this guide. She explained that these standards and indicators were based on effective research practices and would help them to clarify further what they were about to evaluate. She focused their attention on Indicator 6.1—"The language arts and reading program shows evidence that reading, writing, listening, and speaking are integrated processes in the curriculum." The fact that such an indicator was present increased the evaluation committee's confidence in the effort they had undertaken. The committee now had a clear sense of what was to be evaluated.

Collecting the Information

The three characteristics that were selected for identifying an integrated curriculum—more than one skill within a particular assignment, an emphasis on the relationship among different disciplines (e.g., reading, science, social studies), and frequent opportunities for students to develop their reading, writing, listening, and speaking abilities—formed the basis for subsequent evaluation tasks. The next task was to consider different ways an integrated curriculum could be evaluated. Each option had disadvantages and advantages. All of the options had to be examined closely because the evaluation committee had limited resources and a predetermined timetable. (See *Evaluating School Programs: An Educator's Guide*, Chapter 3.)

Choosing an Evaluation Strategy

Four evaluation options were considered: interviews, classroom observations, student work samples (e.g., portfolios), and checklists. After some discussion, committee members rejected interviews because there were too many teachers in the four elementary schools to interview. Not only would the interviews take too much time but there was concern that teachers' recall of what occurred during a particular class might not be accurate. There was also the concern that teachers might overestimate what they actually did so that they would be viewed positively.

Classroom observations and the collection of student work samples would provide detailed information on what actually happened during a lesson, yet the school district did not have the necessary resources to conduct either type of evaluation. To obtain information via classroom evaluations would require the development of an observation measure and the training of personnel to conduct the observations. Before observers enter classrooms, they need sufficient training so that they accurately record what they see. Furthermore, the collection of work samples involved almost as much work as interviews because it would take a considerable amount of time to collect student assignments.

Consideration of the last option, which was using a checklist, caused a lengthy discussion as the evaluation committee were unsure of what would be checked. The first suggestion was to have teachers use a list during their class instruction to check off factors that characterized an integrated curriculum. This option was viewed skeptically because teachers believed instruction was difficult enough to do without having to stop several times to mark a checklist. One committee member, a fourth-grade teacher, suggested that they could examine lesson plans. While this approach wouldn't provide as detailed information as observations or work samples, it would provide the type of general program overview they needed. They could determine which skills were covered, whether assignments extended across different subjects, and the amount of time required to complete a lesson. It might not be possible to determine the specific types of reading, writing, speaking, and listening activities in which students participated; however, given the evaluation committee's constraints (i.e., moneys and time), lesson plans appeared to be the only feasible choice. A checklist using teachers' lesson plans was far less costly than the other three options and could be used with minimal resources and time.

Developing a Sampling Plan

The evaluation committee's next decision was to determine how many teachers' needed to agree to have their lesson plans examined and the number of days they should evaluate lesson plans from any one teacher. This decision was important because instruction differs from teacher to teacher as well as from day to day. They needed to evaluate an adequate number of teachers so that the information represented an overview of what the district's teachers did. They also needed to evaluate enough lessons so that they would have an idea of what average instruction was like in a particular classroom.

To answer these questions, Dr. Goodier listed the number of classrooms by grade and school for the district. (See Table 6.1.) The committee members first noticed that, while there were many teachers in the district, there were not many at any one grade level within a school. This was important because the evaluation committee needed to decide if they were interested in what was happening generally within the district or within each school in the district to implement an integrated reading and language arts curriculum. If they were interested in the former, they could select some teachers at each grade and use information from their lesson plans as an estimate of what occurred across the district. If they wanted to see whether there were differences among schools within the district, they would have to look

TABLE 6.1   Number of Classrooms by School

	Grade Level					
School	K	1st	2nd	3rd	4th	5th
Quinn	2	2	3	3	3	3
Cowesett	3	2	2	2	2	2
Deering	3	3	3	4	4	4
Douglass	2	3	3	3	3	3
Total	10	10	11	12	12	12

at all of the teachers at each grade level in each school. In the latter case, the reason they would have to look at all of the teachers was that there were not many teachers, and any sample group of teachers might not represent the entire group. As stated in *Evaluating School Programs: An Educator's Guide* in this series, whenever there are fewer than 100 persons, it is best to interview each of them. The evaluation committee determined that their task was to discover if there were differences among schools within the district as to their implementation of an integrated reading and language arts program.

Limiting the Scope of the Evaluation

The evaluation committee's next decision was to determine how many days of instruction had to be evaluated. Dr. Goodier asked each teacher to write down how long they believed someone would have to be in his or her classroom to see what typical instruction entailed. They then discussed why each teacher had listed a certain time period. Most teachers believed someone would have to be in their classrooms for 2 weeks, that is, 10 days of instruction. Because no one disagreed with this time period, it was used as the length of time the evaluation committee would use teachers' lesson plans to evaluate whether the reading and language arts program was integrated.

The evaluation committee then looked at sample lesson plans to see what a checklist would include. To estimate how long it would take to evaluate 2 weeks of lesson plans, the committee examined lesson plans from a few of its members. The purpose was to see how committee members could translate information from the lesson plans into a form that others could understand. One thing that became immediately apparent was that teachers provided varying amounts of information. Not all teachers provided a listing of the skill or skills they covered or the time required for a given lesson. Some simply provided the page in the text where the students' assignment was located. If they were to use these lesson plans, they realized they would need to refer to classroom texts to obtain this missing information. Teachers would have to be reminded to include this information during the evaluation period.

Creating the Checklist

Using two lesson plans as examples, the committee quickly listed the number of skills covered during one week across the reading and language arts curriculum, paying particular attention to those lessons during which teachers involved more than one subject area or emphasized more than one skill. Teachers started to voice concerns that this procedure was too complex. They needed a quick way to code the information, and others needed to be able to understand it without referring to a manual. One committee member suggested that they develop a grid that would allow them to visually scan the number of skills covered and the relation between skills by assignment. She further stated that one could simply fill in squares depending upon skills or subjects that were covered. She went to the board and sketched a version of her plan and listened to suggestions about how it could be streamlined. An example of this grid is provided in Table 6.2. Notice how this grid helps you to see what happened by visually showing integration within a day (vertical band of Xs) and across days (horizontal band of Xs). For example, in the first classroom, there were two assignments (top line) across the first 2 days with five skills covered (first two columns). The skills covered in the first classroom on Day 1 were main idea, words in context, and capitalization and they were practiced with one assignment. Also, note how at the bottom of the table the committee marked which subjects were involved: reading, language arts, spelling, and handwriting. Because instruction was provided across subjects and involved more than one skill, this was viewed as indicating an integrated curriculum. This conclusion was strengthened when they viewed Day 2's instruction. The teacher continued with her initial assignment by asking students to write final copies of Day 1's assignment. Because it was a final copy, a greater emphasis was placed on punctuation and spelling so that more skills were included. The teacher had covered a variety of skills with each assignment and had emphasized the relationship among different disciplines.

Gathering the Data

Compare this example with the one presented in the second classroom in which the curriculum was not integrated. On Day 1, there were four assignments, each dealing with a different skill, and none was used across subject areas. On Day 2, students completed an additional five assignments. While similar skills were presented across the two days, they appeared on separate assignments; thus they would not be considered to be integrated assignments. The result is a staircase pattern that continues across the first two days. The evaluation committee members believed the grid would help them and others to see the extent to which teachers were integrating their curriculum. Moreover, they believed this procedure was something they could complete within a reasonable time period without outside

TABLE 6.2   Listing of Skills Covered by Assignment for Two Teachers

	Classroom 1			Classroom 2								
Day	M	T		M	M	M	M	T	T	T	T	T
Assignment	1	2		1	2	3	4	1	2	3	4	5
Skills:												
Main idea	X	X										
Words in context	X	X										
Capitalization	X	X										
Punctuation		X										
Spelling (VCV)		X										
Main idea				X								
Alphabetical order					X							
Cause-effect						X						
Dictionary skills							X					
Predicting outcomes								X				
Verb tenses									X			
Homophones										X		
Multiple meanings											X	
Compound words												X
Curriculum:												
Reading	X	X		X				X				
Language arts	X	X			X				X			
Spelling	X	X				X				X	X	
Handwriting	X	X					X					X

assistance or additional resources. With experience, the evaluation committee concluded that a committee member would be able to code a week's lessons in 15 to 30 minutes depending upon how well documented a teacher's lesson plans were. Perhaps this coding time might be reduced as they gained experience.

The next task was to collect lesson plans from the teachers. It was decided that the evaluation committee members would have teachers in their schools give them lesson plans from the last two weeks. Before they requested the information, each committee member spoke to his or her colleagues at a faculty meeting. They reviewed the reasons for the evaluation and described the progress that had been made. The checklist was explained and an example was provided. At the meeting, they discussed the project and attempted to dispel any doubts about how the evaluation information would be used. To gain further trust, teachers were asked simply to write their building name and grade level on their lesson plans and to cross out any reference to their identities. Teachers were given blank envelopes for their lesson plans. After the results were tallied, their lesson plans were destroyed. Any teacher who did not want to participate was not required to submit plans. Teachers provided the requested lesson plans, and committee members met the following week to code the data. In total, 92% of all teachers submitted their plans.

Organizing and Analyzing Information

To maximize their efforts, the evaluation committee decided to split up into teams based on grade level. The rationale for the grade-level split was that committee members would code the lesson plans from their own grade level more quickly than they could code the lesson plans from another grade level. They split into six three-member teams: Three teams examined K-2 lesson plans; the other three teams examined 3-5 lesson plans. The remaining committee member, Dr. Goodier, was asked to go from team to team to make sure that everyone was using the checklist in a similar manner. Another step the committee used to make sure that the committee members understood how to use the checklist was to have different teams code every tenth lesson plan twice.

Summarizing the Data After the grids were completed, each team counted the number of skills that were covered in the entire week and divided this number by total number of assignments. This procedure provided the average number of skills per assignment. They then counted the number of assignments that involved more than one subject and divided this number by the overall number of assignments to get the average number of assignments that involved more than one subject. To obtain an estimate of how teachers differed, the committee ranked all teachers based on the number of skills presented in a lesson and divided the teachers into three groups (low, medium, and high). This information is presented in Table 6.3.

Reporting Information

Comparing Responses by Grade Level The results showed differences among teachers in how they integrated the curriculum differences that were not related to grade level. For example, teachers in both low groups emphasized isolated skills (hence the 1.0 average) and rarely asked students to complete assignments that involved more than one subject (3% in the low K-2

TABLE 6.3 Percentage of Integrated Assignments for Teachers in Three Groups

Characteristics of Lesson Plans	Grades K-2			Grades 3-5		
	Low	Medium	High	Low	Medium	High
Mean number of skills per assignment	1.0	2.3	7.6	1.0	2.1	6.1
Percentage of multi-subject assignments	3%	10%	45%	4%	12%	52%

group and 4% in the low 3-5 group). These numbers increased slightly when one looked at the medium groups for both grade levels. For example, instead of presenting one skill at a time, the K-2 medium group averaged 2.3 skills per lesson with 10% of the assignments involving more than one subject. The 3-5 group averaged 2.1 skills per lesson and 12% of the lessons involved more than one subject. The low and medium groups at both grade levels had more in common with one another than they did with the high group. That is, the high K-2 group averaged 7.6 skills per lesson and 45% of the assignments involved more than one subject. The high 3-5 group averaged 6.1 skills per lesson and 52% of the lessons involved more than one subject. Compared with the medium group, the high group had a threefold increase in the number of skills per assignment and a fourfold increase in multisubject assignments.

What these results suggest is that teachers in the lowest two groups tend to give assignments that emphasize few skills and fail to integrate the reading and language arts program across the curricula. Because two thirds of the teachers fall into these two categories, the evaluation committee concluded that most teachers were using a standard curriculum approach in the reading and language arts program.

Sharing the Information

Now that the information was collected, the evaluation committee still faced reporting the data. (See *Evaluating School Programs: An Educator's Guide,* Chapter 5.) Committee members discussed the results and what they believed they meant. Dr. Goodier reminded the evaluation committee that their report had to avoid any inferences about which type of instruction was more effective. They simply had to describe what they found and how they found it. She offered to write a draft report for each evaluation committee member to read and provide her with any feedback they believed to be appropriate. After their feedback, the report would be revised as needed and the results shared with various members of the school community. She stated that she would contact Dr. Noyse and show her the results found by the evaluation committee. Next, the results were shared with the principals at their monthly meeting. The principals then shared the results with their faculty. Dr. Goodier apologized for the time this would take yet reminded the evaluation committee that this was a critical stage in their evaluation. They needed to share the results and obtain feedback from their colleagues so that everyone was aware of what their report conveyed. Any misinterpretations at this point might jeopardize the goodwill and hard work that characterized their efforts. Dr. Goodier didn't want teachers to think that one group was necessarily better than another; differences were expected and that was what they found.

Summary of Evaluation Principles

This example illustrated several important principles that should be kept in mind in all evaluations of school programs. As in other examples in this guide, we provide a list of these principles.

1. Do not attempt to evaluate every aspect of the program at once. Focus the evaluation by selecting a few indicators of quality from the list in Resource A and from any other appropriate resources. In this vignette, evaluation committee members used relevant research articles and the standards and indicators in this guide to help clarify their evaluation focus.

2. When choosing a method of data collection, try to select an alternative that minimizes the burden on those who will provide information and can be implemented given your resources and timetable. The task in this vignette was very demanding and the time was limited; thus committee members had to use an approach that was quite involved. Still, much discussion went into which evaluation approach was most appropriate given their resources and time frame.

3. Remember that evaluation often requires hard judgments and negative responses that people might be reluctant to express. If at all possible, design the evaluation in ways that permit those who provide information to preserve their privacy. Always guarantee confidentiality. If possible, provide anonymity. This was especially true in this instance because teachers' lesson plans were being examined. To the extent that teachers viewed the evaluation as having a hidden purpose, they would not be willing to participate in future evaluations.

4. Whenever possible, when the group to be represented is small (say, fewer than 100), collecting information from everyone is better than collecting information from a sample. It is difficult to obtain a representative sample when the group to be sampled is small. Despite the amount of time it took to obtain this information, the evaluation committee asked for lesson plans from every teacher so that they would be sure their conclusions were supportable.

5. When using a checklist, it is critical that the unit of analysis focus on an adequate period of time or events so that it represents an

average of what one intends to measure (e.g., a day's assignments tell you less about what average instruction might be than does a week's). Two weeks of instruction was viewed as appropriate for this evaluation.

6. When using a checklist, make sure everyone agrees on how to define what is measured and uses the same criteria when applying this definition. Moreover, make sure the evaluation committee practices coding what is being examined prior to the formal evaluation. Otherwise, some committee members might code their data inappropriately.

Alternatives to the Strategy Used Here

Although the committee listed different ways to measure the extent to which teachers were integrating the reading and language arts curriculum, additional insights might be gained by reexamining alternatives. For example, if Drs. Noyse or Goodier want to develop inservice activities, they might interview teachers who already are integrating their curricula. Interviews with these teachers as well as observation of their actual instruction would give committee members a better idea about how inservice might proceed.

Cautions Regarding Misinterpretations

There are two cautions that must be emphasized when interpreting these results. First of all, the use of a checklist did not show how effectively teachers implemented their curriculums. What teachers write in their lesson plans and their ability to implement those plans are two different matters. Also, the evaluation did not collect data on how curriculum affects either students' attitudes and performances. Any inference that one curriculum was better than the other cannot be substantiated from these results.

Conclusion

As illustrated in these six vignettes, teachers of reading and language arts and other school personnel can employ relatively simple, straightforward evaluation methods to obtain practical and compelling information to make informed decisions about their reading and language arts programs. Evaluation results can be used to plan a relevant program, enhance specific program activities, document the impact of these activities, and illustrate the need for and effectiveness of the school reading and language arts program.

Lessons From the Vignettes

Effective program evaluation is planned and systematic. Teachers and school personnel in the six vignettes consistently followed a sequence of tasks: identifying specific evaluation question(s), choosing a method of collecting information that will answer the question(s), planning and carrying out a systematic procedure for collecting information, organizing the information in a summary format, and analyzing and interpreting the data summary to answer the evaluation question(s). Such a step-by-step evaluation plan can help ensure that meaningful results, vital to continued support and improvement of reading and language arts programs, are obtained.

Perhaps the most important messages for readers of this guide are the following:

1. Teachers of reading and language arts and other school personnel *can* conduct effective evaluations of their school reading and language arts programs.
2. By conducting program evaluations, teachers of reading and language arts can be convincing advocates for their programs, their students, and themselves.
3. Ongoing evaluations provide vital information for teachers and other school personnel in their continual efforts to improve reading and language arts programs.

Teachers of reading and language arts often must take the lead in educating their many and varied audiences of colleagues, administrators, school board members, parents, and other school personnel about the significance of their work. We offer this guide to teachers of reading and language arts as a tool toward empowerment. With the knowledge and skills to conceive, design, and conduct program evaluations, teachers can improve their programs, secure additional resources, as well as gain the support so vital to continued growth.

Resource A:
Standards and Indicators for Reading and Language Arts Programs

The standards and indicators for evaluating reading and language arts programs listed below are the result of an extensive review of relevant professional literature and a computerized literature search (ERIC). The sources identified in the literature search were augmented by a review of the educational evaluation practices of other states and of professional papers presented at the latest meetings of the American Educational Research Association, the National Reading Conference, the National Council for Teachers of English, and the International Reading Association. We restricted our review to the last 10 years whenever possible. It is important to note that this review was a broad-based review that, in our judgment, reflects the best practices from empirical studies and methods advocated by recognized experts. From this body of professional literature, a comprehensive list of standards and indicators related to reading and language arts programs was compiled.

The initial list of standards and indicators that we developed was quite extensive because the literature on reading and language arts is far reaching. Standards were generic in the sense that they could be applied to programs in reading and language arts at all grade levels. We ultimately recognized that assessment of all the original standards and indicators was not feasible because of time constraints and evaluation costs; therefore the following list contains the standards and indicators based first upon the criterion of importance. In other words, if we judged a standard or an indicator as important, we retained it; if we judged a standard or an indictor as not so important, we deleted it. Indicators that were considered infeasible to measure were also deleted from the original list. Another consideration in developing the final list of standards and indicators was the assumption that program evaluation would occur at the school level; therefore indicators and the procedures and instrumentation that accompanied them had to be sufficiently concrete so that they could be used effectively at that level.

We organized the standards and indicators around the traditional divisions in the language arts, namely, reading, writing, listening, and speaking. These broad headings customarily have more specific content embedded within their respective standards and indicators. For example, embedded within one of the writing standards and indicators are spelling, language usage, language mechanics (punctuation and capitalization), and penmanship. The reading standards and indicators include beginning reading, reading literature and subject texts, vocabulary building, comprehension, as well as learning reference and study skills. Speaking and listening standards and indicators include the use of standard oral language patterns, oral inter-pretation of literature, critical and accurate listening, and other components.

Below each indicator are suggested data collection instruments (shown in italics). Following the list of standards and indicators is Table A.1, which delineates additional data collection instruments and data sources.

Standard 1

Teachers at all levels of a high quality language arts and reading curriculum are well trained and seek opportunities for growth.

1.1 The language arts and reading program shows evidence that teachers have participated in language arts and reading inservice or college-level programs.
Checklists using permanent records

1.2 The language arts and reading program shows evidence that teachers participate in professional language arts and/or reading organizations.
Teacher questionnaire

1.3 The language arts and reading program shows evidence that teachers have preparation in language arts and reading.
Checklist using permanent records

Standard 2

A high quality language arts and reading curriculum provides materials at all levels that reflect a balance among basal readers, information books, literature, computer-based reading instruction, and/or audiovisual materials that students may read and to which they may listen.

2.1 The language arts and reading program provides evidence of a balance of basal reader series, literature, information books, computer-based reading instruction, and/or audiovisual materials.

Materials checklist

2.2 The language arts and reading program shows evidence that students are provided a variety of materials at all levels to read and to which to listen.

Materials checklist

Teacher or student questionnaire

Classroom observation

Standard 3

A high quality language arts and reading curriculum promotes an awareness of the alphabetic principle of the English language, particularly for prereaders, beginning readers, and at-risk readers.

3.1 The language arts and reading program shows evidence of opportunities for prereaders, beginning readers, and at-risk readers to increase phonologic awareness, including awareness of phonemes, onsets, and rines.

Classroom observation

3.2 The language arts and reading program shows evidence of opportunities for prereaders, beginning readers, and at-risk readers to increase orthographic awareness.

Classroom observation

Checklist using lesson plans

Checklist using curriculum guide

3.3 The language arts and reading program shows evidence of opportunities for prereaders, beginning readers, and at-risk readers to learn about the forms and functions of print.

Classroom observation

Checklist using lesson plans

Standard 4

A high quality language arts and reading curriculum provides word recognition instruction that includes phonics, structural analysis, context clues, and sight words.

4.1 The language arts and reading program shows evidence that phonics, structural analysis, context clues, and sight words instruction occurs with connected text.

Classroom observation

4.2 The language arts and reading program shows evidence of direct instruction of sight words.

Classroom observation

Checklist using lesson plans

4.3 The language arts and reading program shows evidence of direct instruction in the structural analysis of words.

Classroom observation

Checklist using lesson plans

4.4 The language arts and reading program shows evidence that direct instruction of phonics is offered mainly in the primary grades, with little instructional emphasis thereafter.

Checklist using curriculum guide

4.5 The language arts and reading program shows evidence of direct instruction in the use of context cues to infer the identity of words.

Classroom observation

Checklist using lesson plans

4.6 The language arts and reading program provides evidence that students are encouraged to reread materials to increase word recognition facility and reading fluency.

Classroom observation

Standard 5

A high quality language arts and reading curriculum includes instruction on specific word meanings.

5.1 The language arts and reading program shows evidence of the use of a variety of instructional methods for teaching specific word meanings (e.g., teaching meanings of affixes and Latin and Greek roots).

Checklist using lesson plans

5.2 The language arts and reading program shows evidence of instruction in the use of context cues to infer word meaning.

Checklist using lesson plans

Classroom observation

Standard 6

A high quality language arts and reading curriculum integrates reading, writing, listening, and speaking as integrated processes.

6.1 The language arts and reading program shows evidence that reading, writing, listening, and speaking are integrated processes in the curriculum.

Instructional record grid

Standard 7

A high quality language arts and reading curriculum includes structured reading activities in which students are actively involved in the comprehension of text.

7.1 The language arts and reading program shows evidence that students know how to use different reading strategies.
Classroom observations
Student interviews
Student portfolios

7.2 The language arts and reading program shows evidence that students know when and why different reading strategies are used.
Student interviews

7.3 The language arts and reading program shows evidence of collected formal and informal diagnostic information on the types of cognitive processes students use when completing various language arts and reading assignments.
Student portfolios
Teacher interviews

Standard 8

A high quality reading curriculum includes unstructured reading activities (e.g., U.S.S.R.) in which students are actively involved in the comprehension of text.

8.1 The language arts and reading program shows evidence that unstructured reading activities are present in the curriculum.
Checklist using lesson plans

8.2 The language arts and reading program shows evidence that students are free to select materials that have the greatest interest to them.
Student interviews
Student questionnaires

Standard 9

A high quality language arts and reading curriculum provides instruction in content area reading.

9.1 The language arts and reading program shows evidence that reading is used by students to learn content and is required in subject areas across the curriculum.
Checklist using lesson plans

9.2 The language arts and reading program shows evidence of use of note taking, summarizing, outlining, and underlining as facilitators to reading and learning content from texts.
Checklist using lesson plans

9.3 The language arts and reading program shows evidence of teaching text structures to facilitate reading and learning from content texts.
Checklist using lesson plans

9.4 The language arts and reading program shows evidence of the use of discussion to facilitate text comprehension and learning.
Checklist using lesson plans

Standard 10

A high quality language arts and reading curriculum recognizes the importance of students' discussing the literature they read or hear so that their understanding, appreciation, and interpretation deepen.

10.1 The language arts and reading program shows evidence that students have had a variety of opportunities to discuss literature, such as conversations, dialogues, small and large group discussions, and interviews.
Checklist using lesson plans
Classroom observations
Student questionnaires

10.2 The language arts and reading program shows evidence that students have had opportunities to be actively involved before, during, and after literature is read aloud to them.
Classroom observations
Student interviews

Standard 11

A high quality language arts and reading curriculum recognizes the importance of understanding the structure of literature genres.

11.1 The language arts and reading program shows evidence of direct instruction in understanding the structures of a variety of literature genres.
Classroom observations
Checklist using lesson plans

Standard 12

A high quality language arts and reading curriculum includes writing as a way to learn content and requires writing in all subject areas across the curriculum.

12.1 The language arts and reading program shows evidence that writing is used as a way to learn content and requires writing in subject areas across the curriculum.
Checklist using lesson plans
Student portfolios

Standard 13

A high quality language arts and reading curriculum includes writing as a substantial and important aspect of the language arts.

13.1 The language arts and reading program provides evidence of the allotment of substantial time to writing.
Time log

Standard 14

A high quality language arts curriculum includes writing as a recursive cognitive and social process that includes planning, drafting, reviewing, editing, proofreading, and evaluation activities.

14.1 The language arts and reading program provides evidence of planning, drafting, reviewing, editing, and proofreading activities.
Student portfolios

14.2 The language arts and reading program provides evidence of prewriting activities as part of planning.
Student portfolios

14.3 The language arts and reading program provides evidence of evaluation and revision activities as part of the reviewing subprocess.
Student portfolios

14.4 The language arts and reading program provides evidence that teachers, peers, and/or others respond to students' plans for their compositions and the drafts of their compositions.
Student portfolios

14.5 The language arts and reading program provides evidence of avoiding excessive attention to correctness early in student writing.
Student portfolios
Teacher interviews

14.6 The language arts and reading program provides evidence that distinctions are made between revising and editing.
Student portfolios
Teacher interviews

14.7 The language arts and reading program provides evidence that students have opportunities to engage in all aspects of the writing process prior to final evaluations of their compositions.
Student portfolios
Teacher interviews

14.8 The language arts and reading program provides evidence that student compositions are evaluated by the most appropriate means, such as holistic or analytical scoring.
Student portfolios
Teacher interviews

Standard 15

A high quality language arts and reading curriculum recognizes that writing assignments are focused to include information about the required voice, topic, audience, and text.

15.1 The language arts and reading program provides evidence that writing assignments are focused to include information about the required voice, topic, audience, and text.
Student portfolios

15.2 The language arts program provides evidence that students write for a variety of purposes, such as to persuade, to inform, to learn, to clarify, to entertain, to express oneself.
Student portfolios
Checklist using lesson plans

Standard 16

A high quality language arts curriculum recognizes that discourse takes many forms, such as essays, reports, journals, summaries, poems, and stories, and has internal structures.

16.1 The language arts and reading program provides evidence that student compositions reflect many forms, such as essays, reports, journals, summaries, poems, and stories.
Student portfolios
Checklist using teacher interviews

16.2 The language arts and reading program provides evidence that student compositions contain a variety of discourse (text) structures.
Student portfolios

Standard 17

A high quality language arts and reading curriculum recognizes that instruction in the conventions of writing, such as spelling, punctuation, language usage, and penmanship, is developed as students are engaged in the writing process, although direct instruction that is developmentally appropriate is provided as needed.

17.1 The language arts and reading program provides evidence that instruction in the conventions of writing, such as spelling, punctuation, capitalization, language usage, and penmanship, occurs as students are engaged in the writing process.
Student portfolios
Classroom observations
Checklist using lesson plans

17.2 The language arts and reading program provides evidence that spelling instruction is developmentally appropriate for students.
Checklist using curriculum guides
Student portfolios

17.3 The language arts and reading program provides evidence that direct instruction in punctuation is provided as needed.
Student portfolios
Classroom observations
Checklist using lesson plans

17.4 The language arts and reading program provides evidence that direct instruction in language usage is provided as needed.
Student portfolios
Classroom observations
Checklist using lesson plans

17.5 The language arts and reading program provides evidence that sentence combining is used to increase students' syntactic understanding and their ability to generate syntactically complex sentences.
Checklist using lesson plans
Student portfolios

17.6 The language arts and reading program provides evidence that direct instruction in penmanship is provided as needed.
Student portfolios
Classroom observations
Checklist using lesson plans

Standard 18

A high quality language arts and reading curriculum includes instruction in listening and speaking skills for comprehensive, critical, and appreciative listening comprehension as well as formal and informal speaking opportunities.

18.1 The language arts and reading program shows evidence that instruction is provided in listening strategies for comprehensive, critical, and appreciative listening comprehension.
Checklist using lesson plans
Classroom observations

18.2 The language arts and reading program shows evidence of the provision of instruction in detecting propaganda and persuasive language.
Checklist using lesson plans
Classroom observations
Teacher questionnaires

18.3 The language arts and reading program shows evidence of opportunities for peer interaction in speaking and listening experiences.
Checklist using lesson plans
Classroom observations

18.4 The language arts and reading program shows evidence of instruction in preparing oral reports, particularly in gathering and organizing information.
Checklist using lesson plans
Classroom observations
Teacher questionnaires

18.5 The language arts and reading program shows evidence of students' storytelling of personal narratives, literature, and content material.
Classroom observations
Checklist using lesson plans

18.6 The language arts and reading program shows evidence that students have had a variety of opportunities to engage in informative language activities, such as conversations, dialogues, and classroom interviewing.

Standard 19

A high quality language arts and reading curriculum includes listening-speaking opportunities that revolve around higher-order and open-ended questions as well as problem-solving tasks.

19.1 The language arts and reading program shows evidence of discussions that revolve around open-ended and higher-order questions as well as problem-solving tasks.
Classroom observation
Teacher questionnaires

19.2 The language arts and reading program shows evidence that students have opportunities to explain the reasoning behind their responses to higher-order and open-ended questions as well as problem-solving tasks.
Classroom observations

Standard 20

A high quality language arts and reading curriculum recognizes the importance of drama in fostering language development, interest, and learning in all areas of the language arts.

20.1 The language arts and reading program shows evidence of the incorporation of a variety of opportunities for dramatic expression and interpretation, such as Reader's Theatre, choral reading or speaking, plays, role playing, puppetry, and dramatization of literature.

Classroom observations

Checklist using lesson plans

20.2 The language arts and reading program provides opportunities for students to view a variety of dramatic presentations and interpretations.

20.3 The language arts and reading program provides opportunities for students to discuss their responses to dramatic presentations and interpretations.

TABLE A.1   Data Collection Strategies for Reading and Language Arts Program Evaluation

Data Sources/ Instruments	Data Contacts						
	Classrooms	Teachers	Librarian	Department Chairs	Assistant Principal	Principal	Students
Records:							
teaching/professional experience		X	X	X	X	X	
continuing education		X	X	X	X	X	
logs/journals		X	X	X	X	X	
observation checklists	X	X					
official program plans		X	X	X	X	X	
annual program reports				X	X	X	
Statements of:							
instructional policy		X		X	X	X	
instructional philosophy		X	X	X	X	X	
Minutes of:							
instructional meetings		X		X	X	X	
staff meetings		X	X	X	X	X	
Plans for:							
program design		X	X	X	X	X	
program implementation		X	X	X	X	X	
Portfolios of:							
class assignments		X	X	X			X
teacher-made tests		X		X			X
student products		X		X			X
instructional materials		X	X	X	X	X	
individual instructional plans (IEPs)		X		X	X	X	
nonachievement outcomes		X	X	X	X	X	
achievement outcomes		X	X	X	X	X	
teachers' lesson plans		X	X	X			
Checklists:							
observational	X	X					X
instructional equipment	X						
instructional materials	X						
Questionnaires		X	X	X	X	X	X
Interviews		X	X	X	X	X	X
Focus groups		X	X	X	X	X	X

Resource B:
Selected References

In developing this guide, we conducted literature searches and examined prominent professional journals. Immediately, we were surprised by the paucity of references to literacy program evaluation studies. Most studies were related to researcher-introduced interventions and not to the evaluation of existing schoolwide programs. As a result, we have drawn references from sources that we believe will be helpful to schoolwide evaluation committees. The references are organized according to whether they provide general information about quality reading and language arts programs, explain the characteristics and procedures that are associated with different evaluation instruments, outline what other states are doing to evaluate their reading and language arts programs, or describe how different evaluation instruments have been developed and implemented by various researchers.

References for High Quality Reading and Language Arts Programs

The following text references were selected to represent a variety of viewpoints and perspectives. They cover similar topics and issues, yet each has its own style and presents different perspectives. Some readers may be more attracted to one text than another—either because they find it easier to read or because they are drawn to its theoretical orientation. We recommend that the evaluation committee study more than one text so that they will be cognizant of different viewpoints and perspectives. Moreover, we would like to state that the following texts are introductory in nature; if the committee needs more specific information, we recommend the use of other texts or professional journals. The selected research articles document the many concerns researchers have about how literacy activities are designed and assessed in classrooms.

Textbooks

Duffy, G. G., & Roehler, L. R. (1986). *Improving classroom reading instruction: A decision-making approach.* New York: Random House.

Gillet, J. W., & Temple, C. (1990). *Understanding reading problems: Assessment and instruction* (3rd ed.). Boston: Little, Brown.

Leu, D. J., Jr., & Kinzer, C. K. (1991). *Effective reading instruction, K-8* (2nd ed.). New York: Macmillan.

Mason, J. M., & Au, K. H. (1986). *Reading instruction for today.* Glenview, IL: Scott, Foresman.

Singer, H., & Donlan, D. (1980). *Reading and learning from text.* Boston: Little, Brown.

Stoodt, B. D. (1988). *Teaching language arts.* New York: Harper & Row.

Temple, C., & Gillet, J. W. (1989). *Language arts: Learning processes and teaching practices* (2nd ed.). New York: Harper Collins.

Vacca, R. T., & Vacca, J. L. (1989). *Content area reading* (3rd ed.). Glenview, IL: Scott, Foresman.

Research Articles

Calfee, R. C. (1987). The school as a context for the assessment of literacy. *The Reading Teacher, 40,* 738-742.

Haney, W., & Madaus, G. (1989). Searching for alternatives to standardized tests: Whys, whats, and whithers. *Phi Delta Kappan, 70,* 683-687.

Johnston, P. (1984). Assessment in reading: The emperor has no clothes. In P. D. Pearson (Ed.), *Handbook of reading research* (pp. 147-182). New York: Longman.

Johnston, P. (1986). Teaching subjects to apply strategies that improve reading comprehension. *Elementary School Journal, 85,* 635-645.

Johnston, P. (1987). Teachers as evaluation experts. *The Reading Teacher, 40,* 744-748.

Johnston, P. (1989). Constructive evaluation and the improvement of teaching and learning. *Teachers College Record, 90,* 509-528.

Neill, D., & Medina, N. (1990). Standardized testing: Harmful to educational health. *Phi Delta Kappan, 70,* 688-697.

Paris, S. G., Lipson, M., & Wixson, K. K. (1983). Becoming a strategic reader. *Contemporary Educational Psychology, 8,* 293-316.

Resnick, L., & Resnick, D. (1990). Tests as standards of achievement in school. In *The uses of standardized tests in American education* (pp. 63-80). Princeton, NJ: Educational Testing Service.

Shepard, L. (1989). Why we need better assessments. *Educational Leadership, 46,* 4-9.

Suhor, C. (1985). Objective tests and writing samples: How do they affect instruction in composition? *Phi Delta Kappan, 66,* 635-639.

Teale, W. (1988). Developmentally appropriate assessment of reading and writing in the early childhood classroom. *The Elementary School Journal, 89,* 173-183.

Valencia, S. W., McGinley, W., & Pearson, P. D. (1990). Assessing reading and writing. In G. Duffy (Ed.), *Reading in the middle school* (pp. 124-153). Newark, DE: International Reading Association.

Valencia, S. W., & Pearson, P. D. (1987). Reading assessment: Time for a change. *The Reading Teacher, 40,* 726-733.

Wiggins, G. (1989). A true test: Toward authentic and equitable forms of assessment. *Phi Delta Kappan, 70,* 703-713.

Wilson, M. J. (1981). A review of recent research on the integration of reading and writing. *The Reading Teacher, 34,* 896-901.

Winograd, P., & Hare, V. C. (1988). Direct instruction of reading comprehension strategies: The nature of teacher explanation. In E. T. Goetz, P. Alexander, & C. Weinstein (Eds.), *Learning and study strategies: Assessment, instruction, and evaluation* (pp. 121-139). New York: Academic Press.

Winograd, P., & Johnston, P. (1987). Some considerations for advancing the teaching of reading comprehension. *Educational Psychologist, 22,* 213-230.

Winograd, P., & Smith, L. (1987). Improving the climate for reading comprehension instruction. *The Reading Teacher, 41,* 304-310.

Wixson, K., & Peters, C. (1987). Comprehension assessment: Implementing an interactive view of reading. *Educational Psychologist, 22,* 333-356.

References for Various Evaluation Instruments

The following books and articles discuss how different evaluation instruments are designed and their recommended procedures. The examples generally are not germane to reading and language arts programs; rather, they cover a wide variety of topics. Several of the references were included in *Evaluating School Programs: An Educator's Guide.*

General

Jett-Simpson, M., Dauer, V., Dussault, N., Gaulke, B., Gerhart, L., Leslie, L., McClain-Ruell, L., Pinlott, J., Prentice, W., & Telfer, R. (1990). *Towards an ecological assessment of reading.* Madison: Wisconsin State Reading Association.

Questionnaires

Robinson, J. P., & Shaver, P. R. (1973). *Measures of social psychological attitudes.* Ann Arbor: University of Michigan, Institute for Social Research.

Shaw, M. R., & Wright, J. M. (1967). *Scales for the measurement of attitudes.* New York: McGraw-Hill.

Checklists

Glaser, B. G., & Strauss, A. L. (1967). *The discovery of grounded theory: Strategies for qualitative research.* New York: Aldine de Gruyter.
Goodman, K. S., Goodman, Y. M., & Hood, W. J. (1989). *The whole language assessment book.* Portsmouth, NH: Heinemann.

Portfolios

Tierny, R. J., Carter, M. A., & Desai, L. E. (1991). *Portfolio assessment in the reading-writing classroom.* Norwood, MA: Christopher Gordon.

References Concerning What Other States Are Doing

In developing this guide, we discovered information that outlines what several states were doing to evaluate their reading and language arts programs. In particular, we've listed technical manuals that were developed by California's educational personnel to evaluate their programs. Other references are from different trade publications and outline various states' efforts to develop alternative assessment instruments.

Technical Manuals

California State Department of Education, Office of School Improvement. (1989a). *Quality criteria for elementary schools* (ISBN 0-8011-0768-7). Sacramento, CA: Author.
California State Department of Education, Office of School Improvement. (1989b). *Quality criteria for middle schools* (ISBN 0-8011-0768-7). Sacramento, CA: Author.
California State Department of Education, Office of School Improvement. (1989c). *Quality criteria for high schools* (ISBN 0-8011-0768-7). Sacramento, CA: Author.

Research Articles

Lewis, M., & Lindaman, A. D. (1989). How do we evaluate student writing? One district's answer. *Educational Leadership, 46*(7), 70-71.
Roeber, E., & Dutcher, P. (1989). Michigan's innovative assessment of reading. *Educational Leadership, 46*(7), 64-69.

Valencia, S. W., & Pearson, P. D. (1986). *Reading assessment initiative in the state of Illinois, 1985-86.* Springfield: Illinois State Board of Education.

Wixson, K. K., Peters, C. W., Weber, E. M., & Roeber, E. D. (1987). New directions in statewide reading assessment. *The Reading Teacher, 40,* 749-755.

References Concerning How Different Evaluation Instruments Are Developed and Implemented by Various Researchers

The following references were drawn from professional journals and describe how different literacy researchers developed and implemented those evaluation instruments that were discussed in this guide. Each reference represents an example of how an evaluation instrument was designed and applied to a classroom setting. The studies focused primarily on reading and language arts programs. In many of the studies, the researchers used more than one measure. Placement of a study into a particular category was based on how well a particular evaluation measured was described.

Checklists

Askov, E. N., & Clark, C. J. (1991). Using computers in adult literacy instruction. *Journal of Reading, 34,* 434-448.

Bergeron, B. S. (1990). What does the term whole language mean? Constructing a definition from the literature. *Journal of Reading Behavior, 22,* 329.

Crawford, J. (1989). Teaching effectiveness in Chapter 1 classrooms. *Elementary School Journal, 90,* 33-46.

Fisher, C. W., & Hiebert, E. H. (1990). Characteristics of tasks in two approaches to literacy instruction. *Elementary School Journal, 91,* 3-18.

Heathington, B. S., & Alexander, J. E. (1978). A child-based observation checklist to assess attitudes towards reading. *The Reading Teacher, 31,* 769-771.

Meyer, L. A., Greer, E. A., & Crummey, L. (1987). An analysis of decoding, comprehension, and story text comprehensibility in four first-grade reading programs. *Journal of Reading Behavior, 19,* 69-98.

Vacc, N. N. (1989). Writing evaluation: Examining four teachers' holistic and analytic scores. *Elementary School Journal, 90,* 87-96.

Interviews

Ganopole, S. J. (1987). The development of word consciousness prior to first grade. *Journal of Reading Behavior, 19,* 415-436.

Meyers, J., Gelzheiser, L., Yelich, G., & Gallagher, M. (1990). Classroom, remedial, and resource teachers' views of pullout programs. *Elementary School Journal, 90,* 533-546.

Miller, S. D., & Yochum, N. (in press). Asking students about the nature of their reading difficulties. *Journal of Reading Behavior.*

Schunk, D. H., & Rice, J. M. (1987). Enhancing comprehension skill and self-efficacy with strategy value information. *Journal of Reading Behavior, 19,* 303-318.

Time Logs

Mason, T. C., & Stipek, D. J. (1989). The stability of students' achievement-related thoughts and school performance from one grade to the next. *Elementary School Journal, 90,* 57-68.

O'Sullivan, P. J., Ysseldyke, J. E., Christenson, S. L., & Thurlow, M. L. (1990). Mildly handicapped elementary students' opportunity to learn during reading instruction in mainstream and special education settings. *Reading Research Quarterly, 25,* 131-146.

Portfolios

Flood, J., & Lapp, D. (1989). Reporting reading progress: A comparison portfolio for parents. *The Reading Teacher, 42,* 508-514.

Paulson, F., Paulson, P., & Meyer, C. (1991). What makes a portfolio a portfolio. *Educational Leadership, 48,* 60-64.

Simmons, J. (1990). Portfolios as large-scale assessment. *Language Arts, 67,* 262-267.

Valencia, S. (1990). A portfolio approach to classroom reading assessment: The whys, whats, and hows. *The Reading Teacher, 43,* 338-340.

Vavrus, L. G. (1990). Put portfolios to the test. *Instructor, 100,* 48-53.

Wolf, D. P. (1989). Portfolio assessment: Sampling student work. *Educational Leadership, 46*(7), 35-39.

Questionnaires

Bean, T. W., Singer, H., Sorter, J., & Frazee, C. (1986). The effect of metacognitive instruction in outlining and graphic organizer construction on students' comprehension in a tenth-grade world history class. *Journal of Reading Behavior, 28,* 153-169.

Hallinger, P., & Murphy, J. (1985). Assessing the instructional management behavior of principals. *Elementary School Journal, 86,* 217-247.

Index